Great Faith

by
Joy Haney

All scripture quotations are from the King James Version of the Holy Bible.

Great Faith by Joy Haney
Published by Radiant Life Publications
© 1992
1st Printing 1992
2nd Printing 1996

Printed in the United States of America

ISBN: 1-880969-02-5

TABLE OF CONTENTS

ACKNOWLEDGMENTS

Thank you and appreciation are deserved by the following persons:

Brent Regnart for his excellent editorial work!

Kevin and Pam Seibold for their support and proofreading.

Nick LeGuern for his fine art work.

Marina Tahod for her excellent calligraphy.

T.R. McDonald and his wife for their contribution of the Foreword.

All the ministers that have imparted faith to me through the years by their anointed preaching. How I appreciate the ministry.

A special thanks to the dear ladies that have prayed closely with me through the years, especially since 1988, when God so marvelously chose to visit us in such a supernatural way. We are one in the spirit, and have been given the spirit of faith that only comes from God; for this I am thankful. To God be the glory for the hundreds of miracles that He has performed through this humble group of prayer warriors.

Special thanks to my husband, Kenneth Haney. He encourages, supports, and is interested in what God has called me to do.

While I am handing out thanks, I want to thank the most Excellent One, my Lord Jesus Christ, who has given me the knowledge and understanding to write. May all praise, glory, honor, and blessing be unto Him for the anointing He has given me and the privilege of being a vessel that He would choose to flow through to bless a needy generation. My heart and soul will ever be grateful to the Eternal God!

DEDICATION

This book is dedicated to my father, T.R. McDonald. When I was a child he inoculated me with faith in our early morning prayer sessions and Bible study. One time when he cut his foot very deeply, he would not go to the doctor. I remember how it bled on the carpet, but he trusted God to heal him, and He did!

Another time, as a new believer, he was working on a bridge some sixteen feet off the ground, and he fell from the bridge to the ground on his back. He jumped up and started shouting, "Hallelujah!" with his hands raised to God, to the amazement of all the workers around him. It was a total miracle!

He has had an attitude of faith in everything he has done. He believed he could get his contractor's license, which some thought he wouldn't, but he did. He always had a positive word to say, and still does. I do not remember him ever being down. When he was going through a trial, I remember him down on his knees saying, "Jesus, Jesus, Jesus," and there close beside him was his Bible open. He loved that Bible more than anything in the world.

He never, never grumbled or complained. It was always, "Just pray--God will make a way." He drove a Sunday School bus for years, and still does. As a child I rode that bus, and I still remember him singing and praising God at the top of his lungs while driving down the road. He always had a smile and something uplifting to say to every kid that got on that bus.

His most recent generous gift to me was the day I called his house and asked him to bring a shovel and help me plant some trees. When he drove up, he was not driving his car. He was driving his truck with the backhoe on the back. Instead of a shovel, he brought a backhoe. At 77 years old, he got on the backhoe and started digging trenches along our backyard, and planted oleanders that they had cut down from their yard. Then he dug holes for the trees. It took us four hours to do what he said would have taken almost a week to do. I told him, "Daddy, the church is using a shovel to get this gospel out to the lost. They need to put the shovel down and get a backhoe."

He is a rare jewel, a prince among men because he is so Christ-like and humble. Whenever his pastor has ever asked anything of the church, he has been right there as one of his most staunch supporters. He is like Abraham in the Old Testament, "and he believed in the Lord..." (Genesis 15:6). He is like Stephen in the New Testament, "...a man full of faith and of the Holy Ghost..." (Acts 6:5).

For almost fifty years now, this man has prayed every day, several times a day. His faith is so staunch in God, you could put him with the most diabolical atheist, and he would make that atheist tremble. He believes God and His word to the fullest degree.

Thank you, Daddy, for the gift of faith that you handed to me as a child. Thank you for teaching me how to pray, and for giving me an intense love for the Bible. Thank you for teaching me God's ways, not only in our Bible studies, but by your superb example. Thank you for teaching me that pride in self alone is stinking to God, but faith in God pleases Him.

Thank you, Daddy, that you raised me on preaching tapes. When many Dads bought their kids a T.V., you bought an old-fashioned reel-to-reel tape recorder. You would set your recorder up at every camp meeting and conference and bring that "gold" home. We listened to preaching much of the time; so much, that I can still to this day preach some of Rev. J.T. Pugh's messages.

In this generation where New Age philosophy, Humanism, Satanism, Eastern cults, spirits of doubt, or whatever is anti-God rears its deceptive head and hollers like Goliath did, God has given me the spirit of David. I can say, "I come to you in the name of the Lord!" and know that God will stand behind His word. I guess I am the richest woman in the world, for I have everything the world is searching for, and I want to impart to them that faith.

Thank you, Daddy, for helping to make me rich in God.

Your daughter,

Joy

Author's note: I am pleased to introduce my Dad, a patriarch and saint, as the writer of this Foreword. He has always had a sense of humor, which you will enjoy as you read his recollections.

FOREWORD

My acquaintance with the author of *Great Faith* is very vivid since she is my daughter. Joy McDonald Haney has always had a "reckless faith." We nicknamed her "Joseph the dreamer," because she was always building big air castles. When just a child she helped baptize our little chickens in Jesus' name, and then expected them to be raised from the dead.

As a teenager she almost drove over the rail on an overpass when learning to drive. When I grabbed the wheel to save us from disaster, she laughed hilariously the whole time. She had faith in her dad that everything was going to be alright. She has transferred that same characteristic of faith she showed in me over to her Heavenly Father.

As a young mother she was speeding her children to school one morning when a red light and siren caused her to pull over. She rolled down the window and said, "Officer, these children cannot be late to school. Their principal is very strict, and he will not allow them to be tardy. Please, follow me." She then proceeded to drive off, leaving him to humbly follow her. They went down

Cherokee Road, and after letting the children off at school she pulled through the school lot and back onto the road. Finally after the officer again turned the siren on, she pulled over. He proceeded to tell her that he could arrest her, and she said, "Officer, my husband is the pastor of this church and the president of that college across the street, and besides I have my bathrobe on." He said, "It does not matter what you have on, and I don't care who your husband is; you do not ever tell an officer to follow you." She very humbly told him she was sorry, and he gave her mercy, but we have had a lot of laughs over this one.

This attribute of confident faith has been carried over into her adult spiritual walk with God. It has been nurtured greatly and channeled in the right direction by much prayer, fasting, and daily study of the Word of God.

When her two-year-old daughter almost drowned and was found lying motionless with her eyes closed, her first thoughts after getting her out of the pool was to pray. After reckless faith revived Angela, her husband and she felt it best to have her checked. The doctor proclaimed it a miracle.

When she started to speak at different districts throughout the United States, she developed a cyst on her neck under her chin which grew slowly to the size of a lemon. She had a specialist check it and he said the only possible way for it to be removed was to cut it out by surgery. Her reckless faith believed God could perform surgery without a knife. At a conference in Missouri where she was speaking, a few ladies joined together and prayed for her. She felt the assurance that God had healed her. It disappeared slowly in less time than it took to grow--without a knife.

As a leader of Ladies Prayer groups in prayer rooms, on the radio, and throughout America and Europe, she has rebuked illnesses such as paralysis, cancer, and others too numerous to mention. She has also prayed for wombs to open, for broken homes to be put back together, and for many other things. God has honored that faith and has been glorified over and over as it is exercised.

God is the author of reckless faith and He can use you or me. He just wants willing vessels to let Him flow through. Anyone can have faith; it is not limited to a few. You will understand and be inspired as you read this book that great faith comes from total trust in God. The Bible says that faith "cometh." It does not just jump on you, but as your faith is exercised it will come and grow gradually. Let your faith soar, for with God all things are possible.

T.R. McDonald

Chapter 1
Great Faith

One cold, sleety, gusty afternoon in December 1942, Jake Skeen, a thirty-year-old Louisiana sharecropper, parked his battered jalopy close to the main gate of Albina Shipyard in Portland, Oregon, just as one of the back tires collapsed with a discouraged groan.

It was a little after four o'clock, and the shipyard lights were turned on in preparation for a dismal night. Skeen got out of the car and examined the flat tire. It was beyond repair, and Skeen stood hunched against the gusts with tears of frustration in his eyes.

In the front seat, his shivering wife stared dully at the wet hulls glistening on the ways. In the back seat, a boy of ten and a girl of six huddled together under a soggy quilt. Beside them, wrapped in an old gray blanket, a ten-month-old baby slept.

This story is excerpted from *Your Prayers Are Always Answered,* by Alexander Lake. New York: Simon and Schuster, c.1956, pp.194-198.

For the Skeens, it was the end of a long, weary trail. They were dirty, damp, hungry, and ragged. They were homeless, penniless, and without ration stamps for gas. They had no hope of shelter against the night.

A gate guard brought the family into the Employees and Public Relations Office, where I told them to huddle close to the electric heater while the guard went to the shipyard restaurant for hot soup and for warm milk for the baby's bottle.

When the guard came back, the baby took its bottle and gurgled happily. The others drank their soup from the bowls in noisy, greedy gulps. My wife Mildred, my assistant, watched them with compassion. I'd seen that look in her eyes many times during the past few weeks, for the plight of the Skeen family was the plight of many families in Portland.

Lured by newspaper ads calling for workers for a group of shipyards, men from all parts of the United States had gathered up their families, and migrated to Portland. Hundreds of them had used their savings to make the trip, only to find when they arrived that there was no housing for them, and no job unless they had money to pay union initiation fees in advance. With no jobs, there was no money to buy welding clothes, helmets, groceries; no money to pay rent for a temporary hotel room; no money to buy gas for the car.

After Skeen learned he could not work in any of the shipyards that had advertised for help, he'd applied for work at other war-industry plants to no avail. The growing number of jobless migrants who showed up at Albina's gates begging for work and enough money to tide them over until they earned enough to finance themselves, rested heavily on officials' hearts.

That December evening as the Skeens crowded close to the heater's glowing coils, Mildred seemed to have reached a decision. She picked up the baby, cuddled it, and said: "Al, there's no decent reason why all these people who come here in such straits shouldn't be given jobs and lent sufficient money to see them in the clear. They're people--they need help. Albina should give it."

"But, Mildred," I said, "we've no jobs. Albina has a waiting list of workers. We're operating at full capacity."

"Jobs will be available," she said, "I've prayed about this, Al. I know I'm right."

"But," I said, "we can't lend Albina's money to just anybody who comes along. We'd lose..."

"Oh, hush!" she said. "Have you so little faith?"

"Well," I said, "I don't feel like assuming the responsibility. We'd have to lend thousands of dollars to stake every destitute family that shows up here."

"Then I'll talk it over with Mr. Erren," she said. And she did.

To my astonishment, Mr. Erren came to our office next morning, put us in his car and took us to a bank where he opened a special checking account and told us to go ahead and lend money as we saw fit.

I called one of Portland's biggest bankers for advice. He said the idea was crazy; he prophesied a loss of from forty to sixty percent. Our auditor was as opposed to the plan as the banker. The superintendent, however, liked the idea, and promised to create jobs for as many as he could.

Opposition to the plan came from other shipyards and from petty officials at Albina. They said the proposed loan was unethical, and would lower workers' morale in the whole area. Mr. Hussa, president of the Albina Shipyard, however, who saw only the good in any situation, said, "Let all the opposition dash itself against the rock of my faith in God and in the goodness of men."

And so began an experiment unique in American industry. Men who did not have the money to buy the right to work, who'd uprooted their families, and had no money to return to their old homes, or to support new ones, were financed until they could stand on their own two feet.

Mildred was no starry-eyed dreamer; she was neither naive nor gullible. She was one of America's outstanding public relations executives. She conducted her departments as she thought Jesus would have her do, and she went ahead lending Albina's money with serene confidence, despite opinions of some minor executives and influential money-changers in Portland.

So the jobless borrowed, hundreds upon hundreds of them. Most were solid citizens who tried to do the best they knew how, but some were pretty questionable characters. They'd enter her office haggard with worry, and leave with faces so alight with relief and gratitude that they seemed transformed.

Bookkeeping records show that Mildred lent in excess of $166,000. Losses? Less than one-tenth of one percent. When the books were closed on the loans, only two men had failed to pay. Both were institutional cases, and Albina forgave the debts.

Morale among Albina workers reached a peak so high that absenteeism dropped from eleven percent to 2.95 percent--the lowest in the United States. Albina workers subscribed a total per man for war bonds that was nine times greater than that of the total per man in any other war plant. Albina workers broke every subchaser-building record. Albina athletic teams won every war-industries sports championship. Albina's flag carried four Navy efficiency stars--an honor accorded no other American shipyard. Because Albina had proved it could accomplish the seemingly impossible, the government appointed this firm its expediter for war materials for 35 other subchaser yards, and for the government's own submarine-building bases.

Said the Secretary of the Navy, Frank Knox, to a meeting of labor leaders in Pittsburgh: "Albina has done as much to improve the morale of the Navy as any other single influence since Pearl Harbor."

After checking the books on Albina's loan set-up, the skeptical banker said: "I admit you've lost less money on loans to workers than we, with all our caution, lost during the same period. You did a good job, but I don't like the way you drag God into it."

Mildred's eyes flashed. "God, not man," she said, "made the laws that govern successful business. When you search for rules that enable you to conduct your business so it thrives, you're really searching for God.

You're seeking to know His will. Obedience to God's rules for business is the only way to lasting success."

This story would have never been written if it were not for the faith of a little woman named Mildred. God gave her the idea; she believed it so strongly that nothing deterred her from seeing it come to pass. Great faith believes when there is seemingly nothing to see or give indication that it can be done. In October 1991, there was a Holy Ghost Explosion at radio station KCJH in Stockton, California, which is explained in the book, *When Ye Pray*. As a result of that experience, the door was opened to the Shepherd's Circle of Prayer to pray on the radio with the listeners who called in their requests. God has miraculously done many tremendous things. One incident that shows great faith on the part of the listener occurred on Wednesday, May 27, 1992 during the prayer hour on KCJH.

A call came in from Fred who requested prayer for his children, George and Michelle. They were getting a divorce and the dad wanted us to pray that God would stop the separation and put the marriage back together. Michelle was in England at the time. The following week, June 3, a call came from Fred again, but it was a praise report. Exactly fifteen minutes after we had prayed in Stockton, Michelle had called from England and said she was coming home and wanted to work her marriage out with George.

This was "great faith" on the part of Fred. He believed that God could work long distance from Stockton to England.

There were two incidents in the life of Jesus in which He referred to people having great faith. What made it great faith? What is the difference between great faith, faith, and little faith?

The first story involves a mother who had a daughter with an unclean spirit. The woman left her house and went to find Jesus and when she found Him she asked Jesus to cast forth the devil out of her daughter. Since the woman was a Greek, Jesus told her that He could not help her because He could only help the Jews. "But Jesus said unto her, Let the children first be filled: for it is not meet to take the children's bread, and to cast it unto the dogs. And she answered and said unto him, Yes, Lord: yet the dogs under the table eat of the children's crumbs" (Mark 7:27-28).

"Then Jesus answered and said unto her, O woman, *great is thy faith:* be it unto thee even as thou wilt..." (Matthew 15:28).

"And when she was come to her house, she found the devil gone out, and her daughter laid upon the bed" (Mark 7:30). The woman was insulted and called a dog, but yet she persisted in her request and answered Jesus back. She did not give up.

The second story is about a centurion and his servant. The centurion went to Jesus and asked the Lord to heal his servant, and Jesus said He would come to his home and heal him.

7

The centurion answered and said, Lord, I am not worthy that thou shouldst come under my roof: but speak the word only, and my servant shall be healed. For I am a man under authority, having soldiers under me: and I say to this man, Go, and he goeth; and to another, Come, and he cometh; and to my servant, Do this, and he doeth it. When Jesus heard it, he marvelled, and said to them that followed, Verily I say unto you, I have not found so *great faith,* no, not in Israel...And Jesus said unto the centurion, Go thy way; and as thou hast believed, so be it done unto thee, And his servant was healed in the selfsame hour (Matthew 8:8-10,13).

Notice the common characteristic in these stories. Each time Jesus called their faith "great faith," it had to do with Jesus healing long distance. In other words, they believed that Jesus did not have to be there in person to heal. They believed that a healing was possible just by Jesus speaking the word. Their faith was so great that the physical presence of Jesus was not required at the scene of the miracle. On both occasions the healing was done before each of them arrived home.

The other times Jesus healed people He commented on their faith, but He did not call it "great faith" because He was present and either He touched them with His hands or they touched Him. There was no touching involved in the "great faith" instances. It was simply healing done via airwaves.

When the woman with the issue of blood approached Jesus and pressed her way through the crowd and reached out and touched Him, Jesus said, "...thy faith hath made thee whole..." (Matthew 9:22). She believed before she touched Him that she would be healed. This is faith.

When Jesus was walking out of the city of Jericho, a blind man, Bartimaeus, called out to him. The people around told him to quiet down, but he just got louder. The persistent faith of Bartimaeus in the face of resistance got the attention of Jesus and the Bible says that "...Jesus stood still..." (Mark 10:49). The Lord asked him what he wanted Him to do for him, and he told Him he wanted to receive his sight. "And Jesus said unto him, Go thy way; thy *faith* hath made thee whole" (Mark 10:52). He believed enough to keep asking even when others told him to keep quiet. He kept crying out even louder, because he knew he would be healed if he could get the attention of Jesus. That is faith: knowing it is done before it is done.

Another example of the difference between great faith and faith surrounds the sickness of Hezekiah. When he was going to die, he prayed and God sent word to Isaiah that he would live.

And Hezekiah said unto Isaiah, What shall be the sign that the Lord will heal me, and that I shall go up into the house of the Lord the third day? And Isaiah said, This sign shalt thou have of the Lord, that the Lord will do the thing that he hath spoken: shall the shadow go forward ten degrees, or go back ten degrees? And Hezekiah answered, It is a light thing for the shadow to go down ten degrees: nay, but let the shadow return backward ten degrees. And Isaiah the prophet cried unto the Lord: and he brought the shadow ten degrees backward, by which it had gone down in the dial of Ahaz (II Kings 20:8-11).

Hezekiah believed, but he wanted a sign, and not just a little sign, but a big one--one that was utterly impossible unless God did it.

You can have great faith, faith, or little faith. Great faith simply believes without a sign or feeling. It believes something is done in another part of the country without having to lay hands on the person or situation. Faith believes it is done, but likes a touching, manifestation, or a sign. Little faith is best described as knowing Jesus can do it, but wondering if He will do it, or believing Him for less than He is able to do. For example, when Elisha was sick unto his death in his older years, Joash, the king of Israel, came down to see him. While he was there, Elisha told him to open the window and shoot an arrow, for they were the arrows of the Lord's deliverance. Then he told him to take the arrows and smite upon the ground. And he smote thrice, and stayed. "And the man of God was wroth with him, and said, Thou shouldest have smitten five or six times; then hadst thou smitten Syria till thou hadst consumed it: whereas, now thou shalt smite Syria but thrice" (II Kings 13:19). How like the king we are sometimes. We let go too soon. Instead of believing God for total victory, we settle for partial victory. Jacob said, "I will not let you go until you bless me." We need to say, "I will not let you go until you bless me with the answer."

When Jesus entered into a ship one day with His disciples, a great storm arose and the disciples thought they were going down. They cried to Jesus to save them. "And he saith unto them, Why are ye fearful, O ye of little faith? Then he arose, and rebuked the winds and the sea; and there was a great calm. But the men marvelled, saying, What manner of man is this, that even the winds and the sea obey him?" (Matthew 8:26-27). They thought He could help them, but after He did the miracle they were shocked about it.

One night the disciples were in a boat in the sea and Jesus started walking on top of the water towards them. The disciples were afraid, but Jesus told them not to be afraid because it was Him and not a spirit as they supposed.

And Peter answered him and said, Lord, if it be thou, bid me come unto thee on the water. And he said, Come. And when Peter was come down out of the ship, he walked on the water to go to Jesus. But when he saw the wind boisterous, he was afraid: and beginning to sink, he cried, saying, Lord save me. And immediately Jesus stretched forth his hand, and caught him, and said unto him, O thou of little faith, wherefore didst thou doubt? (Matthew 14:28-31).

The disciples had no faith, but Peter had a little faith. At least he was willing to get out of the boat and walk on the water. He did the supernatural as long as he did not doubt. Notice the two ingredients that accompany little faith. They are fear and doubt. When Jesus calmed the sea He asked them why they were fearful. When Jesus helped Peter He asked him why he doubted. Two questions that puzzled the Lord--why are you afraid, and why did you doubt? He could not understand how they could doubt and be fearful when He was with them.

Great faith and faith have neither doubt nor fear. Great faith and faith are persistent. They do not give up until they get what they need. When Jesus departed out of a certain city there were two blind men that started following Him. When Jesus entered a house--that did not stop the blind men. They went into the house also without being invited. Jesus asked them if they believed He could heal them and they told Him yes. "Then touched he their eyes, saying, According to your faith be it unto you" (Matthew 9:29). If you believe it strong enough you shall have it.

This generation needs to press in against the great God and see Him up close; for the closer you get to Him the bigger He becomes. Believe God can do anything, for everything is a small thing for God to do. It is time to magnify the Lord by believing in His great power. You think things are impossible? Remember, impossibilities are light things for the Lord God of the universe to take care of--just tiny things for His magnificent power.

In the Old Testament when the land was dry and the people needed water, Elisha heard from the Lord and these were his instructions: "Thus saith the Lord, Make this valley full of ditches. For thus saith the Lord, Ye shall not see wind, neither shall ye see rain, yet that valley shall be filled with water, that ye may drink, both ye, and your cattle, and your beasts. And this is but a light thing in the sight of the Lord..." (II Kings 3:15-18a). He did not need to operate in normal channels, for He could make water come up out of the ground if He wanted to do so. He can do it anyway He wants. He is not bound by our finite conceptions of thought. He is God, and beside Him there is none other.

I have in my Bible the following praise report dated April 3, 1992 that was written down and handed to me.

Sis. Haney, About a month ago I requested prayer and had a handkerchief anointed in a Ladies' prayer meeting. This was for a five-year old girl named Nicole. Some tests confirmed that she had leukemia. She needed to be checked into UC Davis for further testing. Her mother took the prayer cloth with them. We just received news that the doctors concluded there is absolutely nothing wrong with her! It was a miracle, and we thank God! Signed, Vickie.

Who had the faith? No one will ever know, but someone had the faith, because Jesus said according to your faith be it unto you. You can have whatever you have faith for! If faith is placed in the doctor's reports and believed, then that is what is received. As long as there is faith, there is hope. When fear, doubt, and weariness take over the mind, then there can be no miracle. Someone has got to have the faith. This book will explore faith dressed in its many garments. May you take off the garments of doubt that shroud the mind, and wear the garments of faith that will cause you to soar and believe even when the enemy's missiles are fired toward you. When you walk through the dark waters and the fiery furnace, may your faith stay steadfast in God and His word. May your ears be deaf to anything that is contrary to the Word of God whether it be circumstances, man's wisdom, negative reports, or hell's attacks. You can have faith in this day that we live in, and you can walk victoriously even in the midnights and the tormenting difficulties you face.

Upon the authority of the word of God and personal experiences I know that God still raises people from comas, restores people considered clinically dead, and heals cancers, tumors, and diabetes. The list of what we have seen God do is endless. The power of God is still the same. God has not changed--we have-- but faith is available to anyone, anywhere, anytime. It is a gift from God, and He is a good God that loves to give people gifts. Faith is an attitude or a spirit and God and man work together attaining it. This is the day to let God be God! He said, "Yea, before the day was I am he; and there is none that can deliver out of my hand: I will work, and who shall let it?" (Isaiah 43:13).

Chapter 2
Faith Is

When Hudson Taylor, the famous missionary, first went to China, he travelled on a sailing vessel. At one point of their journey they came near some cannibal islands, and the savages were eagerly anticipating a feast as the ship slowly drifted toward an island.

The captain went to Mr. Taylor and asked him to pray for the help of God. "I will," said Taylor, "provided you set your sails to catch the breeze."

The captain declined to make himself a laughing-stock by unfurling in a dead calm. Taylor said, "I will not undertake to pray for the vessel unless you will prepare the sails." So the captain had the crew unfurl the sails.

While engaged in prayer, there was a knock at the door of his stateroom. "Who is there?" asked Mr. Taylor.

The captain's voice responded, "Are you still praying for wind?"

"Yes," answered Mr. Taylor.

"Well," said the captain, "you'd better stop praying for we have more wind than we can manage."

That is faith! "Now faith is the substance of things hoped for, the evidence of things not seen" (Hebrews 11:1). Faith believes it is done before it is done. Faith is not praying, waiting, and then seeing. Faith is seeing before there is anything to see.

George Mueller of Bristol was known as a man of faith. He had over 25,000 answers to prayer during his lifetime. An event that demonstrates his faith in God happened while he was traveling. He was on board a ship that was bound for Quebec. One foggy day the captain of the ship was on the bridge and George Mueller went to him and said, "Captain, I have come to tell you I must be in Quebec on Saturday afternoon."

The captain told him it would be totally impossible! George Mueller simply told him that if his ship could not take him to Quebec by Saturday, God would provide another way. He proceeded to tell the captain that he had never broken an engagement in 57 years, and that he would go downstairs to the chart room and begin to pray.

The captain looked at that man of God and thought to himself, "What lunatic asylum can that man have come from, for I never heard of such a thing as this!" "Mr. Mueller," he said, "do you know how dense this fog is?"

"No," he replied, "my eye is not on the density of the fog, but on the living God who controls every circumstance of my life."

The captain's reflections about the incident was this: "Mr. Mueller knelt down and prayed one of the most simple prayers. When he had finished I was going to pray, but he put his hand on my shoulder and told me not to pray."

"He told me, 'As you do not believe He will answer, and as I believe He has, there is no need whatever for you to pray about it.'"

George Mueller then told the captain to get up, open the door, and he would find the fog gone. The captain did as he was told. Sure enough, the fog had lifted and Mr. Mueller arrived at Quebec on Saturday.

Faith is not believing that God can, but that God will. It is always a war between faith and doubt. Doubt lurks in the corner of your mind making big the circumstances, whereas faith shows God in His majesty and power. Someone handed me the following poem that says it well.

Doubt sees the obstacles,
Faith sees the way!
Doubt see the darkest night,
Faith sees the day!
Doubt dreads to take a step,
Faith soars on high!
Doubt questions, "Who believes?"
Faith answers, "I!"

Faith is believing something into existence. It is substance. It is as real as a tree. Jesus said, "...If ye have faith as a grain of mustard seed, ye shall say unto this mountain, Remove hence to yonder place; and it shall remove; and nothing shall be impossible unto you" (Matthew 17:20).

That same seed can become a tree. Jesus spoke about the kingdom of heaven being like a grain of mustard seed, which "...is the least of all seeds: but when it is grown, it is the greatest among herbs, and becometh a tree, so that the birds of the air come and lodge in the branches thereof" (Matthew 13:32). The grain-of-mustard-seed faith can grow into a tree and crowd out all doubt. The branches can go into your whole consciousness and push out the enemies of faith: men's wisdom and doubt. Paul admonished the church to not stand on men's wisdom. "That your faith should not stand in the wisdom of men, but in the power of God" (I Corinthians 2:5).

Jesus showed the power of faith in Matthew 21.

And when he saw a fig tree in the way, he came to it, and found nothing thereon, but leaves only, and said unto it, Let no fruit grow on thee henceforward for ever, And presently the fig tree withered away, And when the disciples saw it, they marvelled, saying, How soon is the fig tree withered away! Jesus answered and said unto them, Verily I say unto you, If ye have faith, and doubt not, ye shall not only do this which is done to the fig tree, but also if ye shall say unto this mountain, Be thou removed, and be thou cast into the sea; it shall be done. And all things, whatsoever ye shall ask in prayer, believing, ye shall receive (Matthew 21:19-22).

Faith works if you just believe like a child. In August 1989 we had started building a new house. One day in

October I called the building site and the contractor told me that it was raining hard and all the men were talking about leaving. I told him, "Tell them not to leave yet. I'm going to pray."

I opened the door and looked up at the rain clouds and said loudly, "Rain, go away in the name of Jesus!" Then I prayed and said, "God, you are God and nothing is impossible with you. Let the rain stop so we can get the things done now that need to be done before winter sets in. God help us." I kept looking at the sky believing, knowing that the sun was going to break through the clouds. In ten minutes my phone rang and the builder told me that the rain had stopped. I went and looked out again and saw that the sun was beginning to shine through the clouds. I just raised my hands and worshipped the Great God of the universe who heard a sincere prayer in Stockton, California and answered it. Matthew 9:29 was made real to me that day: "According to your faith be it unto you."

When everything is totally opposite of what you are praying for, faith believes anyhow. Faith is not contingent on what is felt, seen, or heard. It is based on the power of God. Jesus said in Mark 11:22, "Have faith in God." Faith sees the invisible, believes the incredible, and receives the impossible.

Faith power works wonders! Jesus' instructions on faith were simple and to the point. He said,

For verily I say unto you, That whosoever shall say unto this mountain, Be thou removed, and be thou cast into the sea; and shall not doubt in his heart, but shall believe that those things which he saith shall come to pass; he shall have whatsoever he saith, Therefore I say unto you, What things soever ye desire, when ye pray, believe that ye receive them, and ye shall have them (Mark 11:23-24).

Mouth, heart, and mind all have to speak the same language. If you say, "I am healed" with your lips, but say with your heart, "I might not make it," you probably will not make it. Faith is not something that you grab once in awhile like a life preserver. It is part of you at all times. It is an attitude. It is more than positive thinking or saying positive things. It is a rock-solid belief that what you pray for, is done. Faith has no questions; it simply believes that nothing is impossible with God!

When Jeremiah was put into prison he wrote these words: "Ah Lord God! behold, thou hast made the heaven and the earth by thy great power and stretched out arm, and there is nothing too hard for thee" (Jeremiah 32:17). He believed even though circumstances were against him. Faith is not only a substance, but it is the evidence. What is the evidence?

While Jeremiah was in prison the Lord told him he would have opportunity to buy a piece of property from his cousin. When the cousin came to him and made the deal, Jeremiah bought it.

And I subscribed the evidence, and sealed it...So I took the evidence of the purchase, both that which was sealed according to the law and custom, and that which was open: And I gave the evidence of the purchase unto Baruch...And I charged Baruch before them saying, Thus saith the Lord of hosts, the God of Israel; Take these evidences, this evidence of the purchase, both which is sealed, and this evidence which is open; and put them in an earthen vessel... (Jeremiah 32:10-14).

Jeremiah never saw the property; all he had as proof of his purchase was a piece of paper. This is evidence.

Two thousand years ago, Christ came to earth and gave His life for a ransom for lost humanity. His blood sealed His evidence. When He ascended to glory, He put His evidence in earthen vessels and on a piece of paper--a book, if you will. The earthen vessels are each of us, and the book is called the Bible. We cannot see the evidence inside of us, but it is there as sure as the ocean.

Faith is like this. It is the evidence of things not seen.

The Bible is evidence, but whether we choose to believe the evidence is up to us. We cannot see Christ or heaven, but we have a piece of paper that says it is so.

What will it be? Do we have to have something that our hands can touch in order to believe? Or can we believe simply because He says it is so? Faith is the *substance,* or that which underlies all outward manifestations. It is the essence of an existent thing. It is the most important part in any existence--the main part. It is solid substantial matter, not visionary or shadowy. It is the basis of deter-minations of realities.

Faith is the *evidence,* or the state of being evident, clear, plain, apparent. It is conspicuous proof. In ordinary usage, the word *evidence* commonly implies more direct or immediate grounds for belief than testimony. What is the evidence? God's word is the evidence. Let us not obscure it or make it shadowy, but approach it innocently as a child. Jesus said, "...Except ye become converted, and become as little children, ye shall not enter into the kingdom of heaven" (Matthew 18:3).

Chapter 3
Bone Faith

Faith has got to get down in your bones. It must pulsate through your body into the very marrow of the bones. Bones are affected by your attitudes. Faith affects the bones, just as a prolonged broken spirit "drieth the bones" (Proverbs 17:22). "...A good report maketh the bones fat" (Proverbs 15:30).

David said in Psalm 35, "All my bones shall say, Lord, who is like unto thee, which deliverest the poor from him, that is too strong for him, yea, the poor and the needy from him that spoileth him?" (verse 10). David said my bones shall talk. What are your bones saying? We used to have a friend of the family that would say, if you asked her how she knew something, "I just feel it in my bones." Bone faith is in your little toe, hand, and brain. It is anywhere there are bones, and that is in your whole body.

Smith Wigglesworth in his book *Ever Increasing Faith*, relates a powerful incident that took place in his life. He said,

"I was called at ten o'clock one night to pray for a young woman who was given up by the doctor and who was dying of consumption. As I looked, I saw that unless God undertook it was impossible for her to live. I turned to the mother and said, 'Well, mother, you will have to go to bed.' She said, 'Oh, I have not had my clothes off for three weeks.' I said to the daughters, 'You will have to go to bed,' but they did not want to go. It was the same with the son. I put on my overcoat and said, 'Good-bye, I'm off.' They said, 'Oh, don't leave us.' I said, 'I can do nothing here.' They said, 'Oh, if you will stop, we will all go to bed.' I knew that God would move nothing in an atmosphere of mere natural sympathy and unbelief.

"They all went to bed and I stayed, and that was surely a time as I knelt by that bed, face to face with death and with the devil. But God can change the hardest situation and make you know that He is almighty. Then the fight came. It seemed as though the heavens were brass. I prayed from eleven to three-thirty in the morning. I saw the glimmering light on the face of the sufferer and saw her pass away. The devil said, 'Now you are done for. You have come from Bradford and the girl has died on your hands.' I said, 'It can't be. God did not send me here for nothing. This is a time to change strength.'

"I remembered that passage which said, 'Men ought always to pray and not to faint.' Death had taken place, but I knew that my God was all powerful and He that had split the Red Sea is just the same today. It was a time when I would not have no, and God said yes. I looked at the window and at that moment the face of Jesus appeared. It seemed as though a million rays of light were coming from His face. As He looked at the one who had just passed away, the color came back to the face. She rolled over and fell asleep. Then I had a glorious time. In the morning she woke early, put on a dressing gown and walked to the piano. She started to play and to sing a wonderful song. The mother, sister, and brother came down to listen. The Lord had undertaken. A miracle had been wrought."

That is bone faith. Wigglesworth in his own words said he would not take no for an answer. He just believed until, but notice the miracle was preceded by four and one-half hours of desperate prayer alone fighting back the forces of hell and death.

There was once a man that had such faith that his bones brought another man to life. Elisha the prophet died, and they laid him in a sepulchre. Later when a band of Moabites were journeying through the land one of their soldiers died. The men stopped to bury him, but when they spied a band of enemy soldiers coming, they just threw the body into the sepulchre of Elisha. When the man touched the bones of Elisha, he revived, and stood up on his feet. When the men looked back at the man they had just thrown into the sepulchre, and saw him now running towards them, I'm sure they started running even faster thinking a ghost was after them.

Men raised from the dead through the power of dead bones is like a fairy tale to some. There are those that feel that kind of faith has left them high and dry. They are like the bones in Ezekiel. The house of Israel made the statement, "Our bones are dried, and our hope is lost..." (Ezekiel 37:11). The Lord told Ezekiel to speak to the bones. Ezekiel said, "O ye dry bones hear the word of the Lord." The spirit of the Lord breathed upon them and they became life again. They stood upon their feet, an exceeding great army.

What the Church needs is a resurrection of bone faith. The spirit of faith needs to breathe new life into every Christian until a great voice will speak hope and faith in the earth. "For with God all things are possible" (Mark 10:27). David said, "...O Lord, heal me; for my bones are vexed" (Psalm 6:2). Vexed bones are a detriment to the purpose of the Church. If she is to evangelize and bring the gospel to all nations, she needs bone faith--healthy bones that speak words of life, not words of despair. Deep-seated bone faith is needed even when it looks like all is lost.

There is an interesting story about a little woman who prayed and never gave up when her husband was captured by the Japanese Army in World War II. They lived in the Philippines close to the place where the Japanese tortured and killed their victims. The family could hear the screams of the tortured day and night. One night she received word that her husband was going to be killed the next morning. The little mother put the five children to bed and began her prayer vigil in behalf of her husband. These are the words of one of her children:

At four a.m., she woke us saying, "The burden has become so heavy I cannot bear it alone. Get up and help me pray for your father." We gathered in a circle around Mother, with the two-month-old baby on the floor in the center. While we were praying we heard footsteps. We were sure the officer was coming for us, and Mother threw her arms around us as far as she could reach.

Suddenly she said, "Those are your father's footsteps!"

"Are you safe?" he asked, pulling the bamboo door back. We lit the lamp and saw his white shirt splattered with blood from those who had stood near him. "I understand now why they let me go," he said soberly. "You were praying."

He told us that he had been the last in a row of ten men. A man had gone down the row, slashing off the head of each with a sword.

"He raised his sword when he came to me, and just as he was ready to bring it down the officer in charge suddenly screamed, "Stop!" Then that officer roared at me, "Go home. Quick, get out of here. Go home."

"Then he dived at me, grabbed my arm and propelled me toward the gate and past the guard as fast as he could--and here I am."

That had been what was happening at the time Mother was so burdened that she got us up to pray.

The family will never know what the officer experienced to make him change the order--but they know why. He could have seen an angel. Whatever it was, it was the result of faith prayer. That mother prayed until, with such a deep faith, she knew her prayers were going to be answered. She did not know how, but she knew they would be.

David said, "My bones cry out that God will deliver me." Her bones cried out that night. She felt it deep inside of her, although she had to war in the spirit for it. Many times we let circumstances shape our destiny, but this should not be so. There is a power which can raise the human soul above all circumstances, but few people use it.

When people are going through difficult times their feelings are as those described in Psalm 107:

> ...they go down again to the depths: their soul is melted because of trouble. They reel to and fro, and stagger like a drunken man, and are at their wit's end. Then they cry unto the Lord in their trouble, and he bringeth them out of their distresses. He maketh the storm a calm, so that the waves thereof are still. Then are they glad because they be quiet; so he bringeth them unto their desired haven. Oh that men would praise the Lord for his goodness, and for his wonderful works to the children of men (Psalm 107:26-31).

This is the power that lifts man up from the pit. Instead of having despair in his bones, it is possible to let faith erase it away and to trust and wait patiently upon the Lord.

Chapter 4
Blind Faith

In the summer of 1959, on one of the hottest days in August, a power failure in New York City shut off air conditioners, fans, and other electrical equipment in hundreds of apartments and offices. Particularly hard-hit were workers on the upper floors of many buildings, who were in pitch-black offices with no elevators running.

In one of these buildings the problem was solved by a unique method. When darkness hit the guild for the Jewish Blind, the two hundred blind workers, who knew every inch of the building by touch, led the seventy help-less sighted workers down the steps and onto Broadway.

There are too many Christians that see and know too much to the extent that they cannot believe God for a miracle. They have memorized the doctor's report and it sings in their brain. The finances have been analyzed from every direction, and there is seemingly no way that the mess can be straightened out. Everything that is seen is negative, and with the analytical brain working it is impossible to become blind to the impossibilities that surround them. They see and know too much. In their mind there is no way out.

A man named Abraham was living a normal life when one day God appeared to him and told him to get up out of his own country and leave his kindred and his father's house. "Just leave it all behind, and I will lead you to another land which I will shew you in the future," the Lord instructed him.

Did Abraham do such a foolish thing? Yes. "So Abram departed, as the Lord had spoken unto him" (Genesis 12:4). This is what you call blind faith--going someplace simply because God spoke it, not knowing even where you are going. Walking in a direction that has not been mapped out on paper, just walking step by step towards a destination unknown.

The key to this kind of faith is illuminated in an instance when God spoke some strange things to Abraham. God said to Abraham, "Look now toward heaven, and tell the stars, if thou be able to number them: and he said unto him, So shall thy seed be" (Genesis 15:5). Notice the very next phrase, "And he believed in the Lord" (Genesis 15:6). There is the clue.

He did not question the absurdity of the statement God made; he believed. Science will tell you it is impossible for a one hundred-year-old man to have a child and especially for a ninety-year-old woman to bear a child, but Abraham was blind to science, only seeing the power of God.

Blind faith! Simply believing when there are no road maps, no apparent signals and nothing to go on but a voice.

How did he do it? "By faith Abraham, when he was called to go out into a place which he should after receive for an inheritance, obeyed; and he went out, not knowing whither he went" (Hebrews 11:8). He did not know where he was going. He was like a blind man in the fact that he could not see in the natural, but he could see in the spiritual.

"By faith he sojourned in the land of promise...For he looked for a city which hath foundations, whose builder and maker is God" (Hebrews 11:9a-10).

"Abraham, where you going today?" asked one of the neighbors.

Abraham shrugged his shoulders and pointed off into the far distance and said, "I don't really know where I'm going. I just know I'm going."

The neighbor tried to hide the sneering laughter and made some lame remark to cover his confusion. "Well, I hope you find where you're going, because if you don't know where you're going, how will you know you're there, when you get there?"

Abraham remarked, "I know it seems strange for me to leave my house, my kindred, all my family, and everything that is dear to me, but you don't understand. God has spoken to me, and I must obey Him. It is like a radar that is leading me into paths I myself am not even aware."

The neighbor scratched his head and tried to figure out his neighbor's strange behavior, but for the life of him, he could not figure it out. He had looked at it from every angle, and it just did not make sense.

Then when that same neighbor received word several years later that Abraham was going to have a child, he did double up and laugh hilariously. "You've got to be kidding, why Abraham is almost a hundred years old now!" he said.

The difference between the neighbor and Abraham was that one could see and the other was blind. The neighbor could see the impossibilities, but Abraham was blind to them. He could only see God. Yes, both men saw, but they saw different things. Everyone sees, but what they see is the important thing. You must be blind to the apparent things, and able to walk blindly by faith at God's promise.

And being not weak in faith, he considered not his own body now dead, when he was about an hundred years old, neither yet the deadness of Sarah's womb: He staggered not at the promise of God through unbelief; but was strong in faith, giving glory to God; And being fully persuaded that, what he had promised, he was able also to perform (Romans 4:19-21).

He was so strong in faith that he did not even give consideration to the deadness of his body or of Sarah's womb. No consideration! This is the problem among people today. They give too much consideration to lab reports, rebellious kids, the lack of money needed to pay the bills, and any number of things. Consideration is the problem.

Consideration is "careful or sympathetic thought towards something; attentive respect, appreciative regard, a matured thought towards an idea or circumstance; placing importance or giving notice to anything we esteemed important." Abraham did not even consider the impossibility. He considered only God.

It is time to quit considering everything that is coming against you. Throw out the mature thoughts that have ripened in your brain until they have become set in cement. Blindly face anything with the Word of God, not with the word of the doctor. Be fully persuaded, not doubting, that God is able to perform-- not only able, but that He will.

Sarah was not to be outdone by Abraham. "Through faith also, Sara herself received strength to conceive seed, and was delivered of a child when she was past age, because she judged him faithful who had promised" (Hebrews 11:11).

She did not lag her feet in faith. Oh, she laughed at first, but that was just her natural reaction. When she got to thinking about God, she reversed her laughter of disbelief with the laughter of joy. She was a partner to Abraham's "crime" or blind faith, for there were some that thought they were almost committing a crime. It is not normal to do what they did. It was unorthodox, untraditional, and crazy in some people's eyes. It may have been crazy, but the "crazy" ones were the ones that received the promise.

Sarah herself received strength because she judged him faithful who had promised. Everyone makes a judgment call every day. We judge God to be faithful or unfaithful by how much we believe in Him. We tie His hands or loose Him by our faith. There is no question about His power; the question is, "Do we believe Him enough to allow Him to do it?"

Isaiah, the prophet, penned the words of the Lord God. "Yea, before the day was I am he; and there is none that can deliver out of my hand: I will work, and who shall let it?" (Isaiah 43:13). The question is, "Who will let God perform? Who is willing to walk blindly into a miracle?"

When Jesus tried to do miracles in His own country one day, the people asked, "Is this not the carpenter's son?" They could see only the son of a carpenter instead of the Son of God. They tied His hands because of their unbelief. "And he could there do no mighty work, save that he laid his hands upon a few sick folk, and healed them. And he marvelled because of their unbelief" (Mark 6:4-5).

Unbelief has kept many miracles in the incubation stage, for every impossible situation is the seed-bed for a miracle. People say they believe God can do anything, but then they talk incessantly about their ritual of pills the doctor has them on. Their conversation revolves around the gory details of the disease and those that have died with it. That is not faith, that is doubt. Faith refuses to consider the apparent. It believes only in the power of God.

When God promised the children of Israel that they would inherit the land of Canaan, they were excited about it, but there came a test of faith on their part. Moses sent twelve spies into the land to give him a report on how to take it, and ten of those spies came back full of doubt. They did not see God, they saw the giants.

Finally, after the dialogue between Caleb, Joshua, and the people came to an end, God spoke. "And the Lord said unto Moses, How long will this people provoke me? and how long will it be ere they believe me, for all the signs which I have shewed among them?" (Numbers 14:11).

God was actually saying, "What do I have to do to get them to believe? I made a huge body of water roll back and changed it from a liquid state into a solid wall. The floor of the sea was muddy, slippery, and squashy, but I made it dry. I sent them quail. I sent them manna. They saw the plagues I put upon the Egyptians. I brought them from bondage into freedom. Are they so dense to think that I, the God of the Universe, cannot handle a small country of people that appear to be giants?"

Instead of having blind faith, they became blind to the power of God. It is best portrayed in Bernard Shaw's play, *Saint Joan,* in the Epilogue. Here was the scene:

It was 25 years after the burning of the Maid. The curtain rose on the bed-chamber of King Charles the Seventh of France, who, at the opening of the play, was the none-too-bright Dauphin. The spirits of those who played a part in the trial and burning at the stake of Joan were entering the King's chamber. Among them was an old rector, formerly a chaplain to the Cardinal of Winchester, a little deaf and a little daft. He had gone somewhat crazy from brooding over the burning of Joan, but insisted that the sight of that burning had saved him.

"Well you see," he said, "I did a very cruel thing once because I did not know what cruelty was like. I had not seen it, you know. That is the great thing: you must see it. And then you are redeemed and saved."

"Were not the sufferings of our Lord Christ enough for you?" asked the Bishop of Beauvais.

"No," said the old rector. "Oh, no, not at all, I had seen them in pictures, and read of them in books, and been greatly moved by them, as I thought. But it was no use. It was not our Lord that redeemed me, but a young woman whom I saw actually burnt to death. It was dreadful. But it saved me, I have been a different man ever since."

Poor old priest, driven astray in his wits by the haunting memory of his youthful inability to see what cruelty is like without watching a maid burn slowly to death at the hands of her executioners, a man who had to wait for events to educate his judgments!

The Bishop of Beauvais looked at him pityingly and, with infinite pathos in his voice, cried out, "Must then a Christ perish in torment in every age to save those that have no imagination?"

Notice the phrase, "a man who had to wait for events to educate his judgments." The death of Christ on the cross was not enough, he had to see with his own eyes the death of a follower of Christ. He had no faith or imagination to simply believe, but he was blind to the evident. Instead of having blind faith and believing, he became blind to the magnificent power of Christ.

Just as the Bishop was asking, "Must there be a Christ or a semblance of Christ die in every age for man to believe?", God was asking Moses, "What must I do to make them believe in My power? Can't they just believe because of what has already happened in the past?"

You will make a judgment call today. You will do as Abraham did and simply believe, or you will refuse to believe and miss out on all the blessings that came upon Abraham. What are you blind to--God's power or your circumstances? Walk blindly in the direction of the miraculous and it shall come to pass.

Chapter 5
Eye Faith

One beautiful midsummer morning a young man arose from a long night's sleep, stretched, and dressed in a hurried manner. He wanted to get his walk in before the day began. He strolled through the door and was not outside too long until he strolled right back inside. He went out leisurely, but came back in rather breathlessly.

His eyes were bulging, the veins in his neck were popping and his face was quite pale. As he ran to his master he said, "...Alas, my master! how shall we do" (II Kings 6:16). He had just seen horses, chariots, and a great host surrounding the whole city of Dothan.

Elisha simply said, "Fear not; for they that be with us are more than they that be with them" (II Kings 6:16).

As shown here, when fear is present the thing to do is pray. That is what Elisha did. He prayed, "Lord, I pray thee, open his eyes, that he may see. And the Lord opened the eyes of the young man; and he saw: and, behold, the mountain was full of horses and chariots of fire around about Elisha" (II Kings 6:17).

AND HE SAW! What powerful words. Nothing changed except his vision. God was there all the time to do the impossible. The servant just could not see. He had eye problems as many Christians do today. They see what is apparent, but they do not see the invisible forces working for them. Faith sees the invisible, believes the incredible, and receives the impossible.

Can you imagine the scene in your mind? The city surrounded by horses, chariots and a great host, but behind them in the mountains were fire, horses, and chariots driven by angelic hosts totally unseen by everyone but Elisha. He saw with the eye of faith the things of God.

This is not the kind of faith that has to see to believe such as Thomas had. Thomas said, "Except I shall see in his hands the print of the nails, and put my finger into the print of the nails, and thrust my hand into his side, I will not believe" (John 20:25).

Thomas could not even believe if he saw. He had to feel also. Seeing and feeling the hands were not enough. He had to have further proof by checking His side also. The mentality of faith he had is appalling. It grieved Jesus and eight days after Thomas had made his faithless statement, Jesus appeared to the disciples and the one Jesus addressed was Thomas. Jesus told him to touch and feel. That was on His mind and He wanted to help increase the faith of Thomas. After this encounter with Jesus, Thomas fell on his knees and cried, "Jesus, my Lord and my God."

It was then Jesus emphasized the power of eye faith. He said, "...Because thou hast seen me, thou hast believed: blessed are they that have not seen, and yet have believed"

(John 20:29). Eye faith sees when there is nothing to see: no proof! Eye faith does not have to see fleshly things to believe as in the case of Thomas. It does not believe what it sees with the fleshly eyes as in the case of Elisha. It believes what it sees in the spirit realm, or what "thus saith the Lord."

There was a little mother that had this kind of faith. For many years the mother of Tom Carter prayed that God would save her boy and make a preacher out of him. Her boy became very wicked and landed in prison, but the mother just kept praying and believing. One day she received a telegram from the prison saying that her son was dead.

That mother was stunned for a few minutes. Then she went to her room, and spread her Bible out on the bed. She prayed, "O God, I have believed the promises Thou didst give me in Thy Word. I have believed that I would live to see Tom saved and preaching the gospel. Now, a telegram says he is dead. Lord, which is true, this telegram or Thy Word?"

She then got up off her knees and sent back her own telegram. "There must be some mistake. My boy is not dead." And she was right. There was a mistake, and when he was released from prison, her boy became a soul-winner and preacher of the Gospel. She refused to believe what her eye saw. She believed what the Lord had promised her. She saw her boy saved before he was saved. A yellow piece of paper with words of doubt written on it did not change her faith or her vision. She refused to believe anything other than the fact that her boy was going to be saved, for in her mind nothing else was true.

Faith does not wait and see if it happens. Faith sees before it happens. Paul told the Ephesians how he prayed for them. He prayed,

> That the God of our Lord Jesus Christ, the Father of glory, may give unto you the spirit of wisdom and revelation in the knowledge of him; The eyes of your understanding being enlightened; that ye may know what is the hope of his calling, and what the riches of the glory of his inheritance in the saints, And what is the exceeding greatness of his power to usward who believe; according to the working of his mighty power (Ephesians 1:17-19).

He is praying as Elisha prayed, "Lord, open their eyes and let them see." To see the results and then believe is not faith. Faith sees before it is done. When God says it, faith simply believes even if it sounds absurd. It is best described by a Norwegian story of a young man dressed in a sweater and overalls who entered a car dealer's shop just north of the Arctic Circle. He asked if there were very many cars in stock and was told there were many.

He simply said, "I want sixteen cars, if I like the model."

The salesman brushed him off saying, "I have no time for jokes. Buzz off."

Well, he did, right across the street to another car dealer selling a different make of cars.

He made similar inquiries and got full service. The man in overalls really did want sixteen cars and paid in cash. He belonged to a Norwegian trawler that caught record quantities of herring that season. All the fisherman decided to buy new cars for themselves. They wanted to buy all sixteen at once, to get the highest possible discount.

God says something in his Word, and sometimes we take it as a joke because it sounds too good to be true. We do not laugh about it because we are hurting so, but we do not take it seriously because the situation we are in is so devastating and impossible. We question how, instead of believing. Instead of releasing, we grieve and carry our burden around instead of praising God in faith that it is done. We have difficulty seeing someone healed when the symptoms are still there. I have been there many times and I am convinced that except faith be present there can be no healing. As Jesus told the blind men in Matthew 9:29, "According to your faith be it unto you."

In 1986 I noticed a small growth that started growing under my chin area on my upper neck. I went to Dr. Westafer and he checked me, inserting a needle into it for further testing. Then he sent me to the hospital for x-rays. When I went back to visit him he said I would have to go to Dr. Goldberg for surgery. I asked him if there was any medicine that could dissolve the growth, and he looked me in the eye and said, "Nothing but surgery will take this away."

I left the following week to go speak at the Missouri District Ladies Retreat and because of the tests the growth was very ugly and swollen. Several ladies remarked about it and a group of ladies prayed for me. When they finished one minister's wife made the statement, "The work is done."

I said, "O.K. I accept that from the Lord. I am healed in Jesus' name."

When I went back home, I told everyone I was healed, but the growth was still there. Several times someone would say something about it, and I would say, "I am healed. You just watch this thing--it will be gone."

One lady came up to me and asked, "Isn't that lying--to say that you are healed when the growth is still there?"

I answered her, "No, it is not lying. It is faith; for you see, I am healed. You just can't see it yet, but you keep watching and you will see this thing disappear."

Every day I would pray and praise God for my healing. At one point I looked at the growth in the mirror and I said, "I curse you in the name of Jesus. You have to go because the blood is applied on you."

Sure enough, after three months the growth disappeared and the proof of my healing was made known to all. Down deep I knew I was healed that day in Missouri, but many others could not believe because they were able to only see in the fleshly realm. By God's grace and power He let me see my healing the day the minister's wife said the words, "The work is done."

When I finally went back to Dr. Westafer, he looked at me with surprise and asked me what I had done. I said, "Dr. Westafer, we prayed and God healed me."

He jokingly said, "I'm going to have you come and pray for all my patients."

When I went back to him the first time after the tests he gave me the x-rays and the Stockton Radiology Medical Group report plus instructions to take with me to Dr. Goldberg, the officiating surgeon. I kept them and every so often I get them out and thank God for one of my many miracles. Here was their official report:

The lateral view best demonstrates a soft tissue density present in the anterior upper neck below the chin. I do not identify any calcification within the mass. It is difficult to optimally measure, but it probably measures up to 3.5 cm. or so in size. The frontal view is somewhat light in technique but shows that the mass extends to the left of the midline. IMPRESSION: There is a large soft tissue mass in the upper neck below the chin without any calcification or identifying characteristics. *R.G. Schwemley, M.D.*

Eye faith sees the spirit at work doing the impossible before the natural eye sees the results. It is simply believing in the supernatural work of God even in the face of impossibilities. The Psalm says it for all of us, "Open thou mine eyes, that I may behold wondrous things out of thy law" (Psalm 119:18). The wonder is in the scripture. Just help us to believe it, Lord.

Ezekiel 12:2 describes it well when he says they have eyes to see, but they see not. Jesus talked about it in Matthew 13. He said,

...because they seeing see not; and hearing they hear not, neither do they understand. And in them is fulfilled the prophecy of Esaias, which saith, By hearing ye shall hear, and shall not understand; and seeing ye shall see, and shall not perceive: For this people's heart is waxed gross, and their ears are full of hearing, and their eyes they have closed; lest at any time they should see with their eyes and hear with their ears, and should understand with their heart, and should be converted, and I should heal them. But blessed are your eyes, for they see; and your ears, for they hear (Matthew 13:13-16).

He blessed the eyes of faith that could believe for Him to heal them. It is not just a fairy tale. It is not a tradition. It is live pulsating power readily available to those that can see with the eye of faith.

If you are blind spiritually as the blind man from Bethsaida was, just come and ask Jesus to touch your spiritual eyes. Jesus spit on his eyes and put His hands on them and asked him what he saw. The blind man answered, "I see men as trees walking" (Mark 8:24). You may be beginning to see, but only as in a blur. Let Jesus again put His hands on your eyes and do what Jesus told the blind man to do. Jesus made him look up. Faith looks up, doubt looks down, and worry looks around. Quit looking around, or down, and look up. Notice the Bible says when the blind man obeyed and looked up, he saw clearly. Clear eyesight only comes by looking up away from the problem unto God.

When Hagar and her son were sent away into the wilderness with only a jug of water and a loaf of bread, they both just lay down and wept. God always hears tears, and He responded. He said to Hagar, "Fear not; for God hath heard..." (Genesis 21:17). "And God opened her eyes, and she saw a well of water; and she went, and filled the bottle with water, and gave the lad drink" (Genesis 21:19). When God opened her eyes, then she saw the well of water. Her troubles blinded her until God let her see. God always gives a well, not just a bottle. He always gives more than enough!

Chapter 6
"It Is Well" Faith

The hot sun beat down upon the heads of the Shunammite men working in the fields nestled among the low hills which bordered the valley. A small lad who had grown old enough to accompany his father to the field was seen playing over to one side. Suddenly those watching him noticed him grabbing at his head. Running to his father, he cried, "My head, my head," as if in great pain. The father, who was busily reaping the grain, turned to a young teenage lad and said, "Carry him to his mother."

The young boy picked up the suffering child and carried him to the little humble home on the narrow brick street in the village of Shunem not far from the fields. The mother of the child, just returning from the market, saw the young boy carrying her son and was filled with alarm. She quickly put the morning purchases of fresh vegetables on the table and while taking her boy in her arms asked what was wrong.

"His father asked me to bring him home when his head started hurting," replied the young man.

The mother carried the child over to the rocker and rocked her boy until noon and then he died. She immediately went upstairs and laid him on the bed of the man of God, Elisha. Shutting the door behind her she went out. She then called to her husband and asked him to send her a donkey and a young man so she could go visit the man of God.

Her husband asked in perplexity, "Why? It is neither new moon, nor sabbath."

She simply answered with words of great faith, "It shall be well."

She was a strong, courageous woman with an aching heart, but her faith was bigger than her hurt. She saddled that donkey to a cart and then said to the servant, "Drive, and go forward: slack not thy riding for me, except I bid thee" (II Kings 4:24). Her attitude was victory--no retreat! Drive straight into the winds of adversity. Look neither to the left nor to the right. Do not let up until we get to where we are going.

When that determined little woman got to Mount Carmel the man of God saw her afar off and told his servant, "Behold, yonder is that Shunammite. Run now, I pray thee, to meet her, and say unto her, Is it well with thee? is it well with thy husband? is it well with the child? And she answered, It is well" (II Kings 4:26).

She passed Gehazi and went straight to Elisha and fell down and grasped his feet. Gehazi tried to thrust her away, but Elisha said, "Let her alone. Something terrible is wrong."

The little woman said, "You told me that I would have a son and I told you not to deceive me."

That was enough for Elisha. He knew then what was wrong. He told Gehazi to take his staff and go lay it upon the face of the child and to hurry up about it.

The mother of the child said, "Oh, no! As the Lord liveth, and as thy soul liveth, I will not leave thee" (II Kings 4:30).

What could Elisha say to that? He simply did as she said and followed her. Gehazi had already left and was running to the house where he arrived panting for breath. He ran up the stairs and laid the staff on the child, but nothing happened. Then he ran back and told Elisha the child did not wake up.

"And when Elisha was come into the house, behold, the child was dead, and laid upon his bed" (II Kings 4:32). What did Elisha do? He prayed. The Bible does not say how long he prayed, only that he prayed. Then his prayer took action. He went in and lay upon the child, put his mouth upon his mouth, his eyes upon his eyes, and his hands upon his hands and the child waxed warm. Elisha got up and walked around in the house and then went back up and stretched himself on the child a second time. That time the child sneezed seven times and opened his eyes.

Then all was well just as the mother had said it would be. How many mothers would have told their husbands everything was going to be alright when their child lay dead on the bed? Can you get a grasp of this kind of faith? These were not empty words when she said, "It is well." She really believed what she was saying.

She could have wept and wailed and nobody would have condemned her for it. That was the normal thing to do, but she was not normal. She was a humble woman of faith. Humble enough to believe for a miracle even when the elements were against her. Humble enough to buck traditions and defy protocol.

Notice when she received her miracle, she did not strut saying, "Look at my great faith." Instead, she fell at Elisha's feet and bowed herself to the ground. The reason why she could have faith is because her eyes were not on herself. They were on the God of Elisha. She believed in God more than she believed in death. You have a choice to be normal or you can join the forces of the Shunammite woman and believe in God with your heart so forcefully that it blinds you to circumstances.

There is a clue to her attitude of humility. Notice in verse 13, after she and her husband had made a prophet's chamber for Elisha in her home that Elisha wanted to do something for her. Elisha asked if she wanted to be known. He said, "Do you want me to talk to the king about you and tell him what you have done?"

She simply answered, "I dwell among mine own people." Eloquent moving words that spoke volumes about her character. She was a woman of loyalty, kindness, and love. Those six words paint a picture of her. As her kind heart was instrumental in helping the prophet's chamber to come into being, so she treated other people of the village with the same concerned care.

She always had a helping hand outstretched to her neighbor, friends, and family. She was a woman who cared deeply and gave richly. She believed not only in God, but in people. She was a woman of faith in every avenue of her life. It was an ingrained attitude that pulsated through her veins and waltzed in the corridors of her brain.

She was born among her people, she had walked among her people, and she would die among her people. No royal attention was to be desired, no special gifts did she ask. "Just let me serve and do for others as I have always done" was her answer.

God always honors faith and humility. He said the humble would be exalted. It is the humble who have faith to believe because they decrease in their own confidence and belief in their intellect. The wisdom of men and the apparent impossibility of a situation do not sway them because they are plugged into infinity or God Himself. Those who believe become as little children and humble trust replaces cynicism, believing that with God all is well!

One morning in the Shepherd's Circle of Prayer we had a director of a pre-school and day care come into the prayer meeting with a stack of papers. She related how the state had insisted that the center owed the state $6,000.00 in back money. The director explained to them that this was a mistake, but to no avail. The state would not listen, and so the day care worked out a plan where they would send in $200.00 a month to pay this debt. She asked us to lay hands on all the papers that represented funds owed to them by parents that were behind in their bills. The center was struggling and needed a miracle.

The ladies gathered around and earnestly prayed that God would send His angels to the state capitol and erase the bill from the computer, and that all the parents who owed money would be blessed so they could pay the center. When we got through praying, one of the ladies said with a big smile, "All is well. The Lord has already taken care of it." We left with faith in our hearts knowing that God was bigger than money, circumstances, or hardheads.

It was two weeks later that the director of the pre-school had sent in the scheduled $200.00 to apply towards the bill the state said they owed. Within a short time she received a letter from the capitol saying that the pre-school did not owe the money and enclosed was the $200.00 check. So the director called and inquired about it, and the secretary searched the computer for the files and there was not one thing in the computer concerning the $6,000.00 bill. The center had been making the payments for several months, so it had been in there previously. When the director came back to the prayer meeting and gave the praise report of how the Lord had sent His angel and erased the bill from the computer, a great praise ascended to the throne of God. He is able to do exceeding, abundantly above what man asks or thinks. God definitely made it well. The bill was not owed in the first place, so He just erased it.

Faith can do anything. It can make a diseased mind well. When you go to church, hear the Bible read, and listen to the sermon, sound waves fall upon your ear and spiritual ideas are transmitted to your brain. It makes contact with the thought of fear and the more powerful thought starts healing the diseased thought.

This is why it is so important to put Joshua 1:8 into action.

This book of the law shall not depart out of thy mouth; but thou shalt meditate therein day and night, that thou mayest observe to do according to all that is written therein: for then thou shalt make thy way prosperous, and then thou shalt have good success.

This scripture involves speaking, thinking, and obedience.

Do this every day and your life will change. Get up in the morning and pray before leaving your house. Read a positive scripture and write it on a piece of paper and take it with you. Look at it throughout the day, memorize it, and think on it. If you do this every day you will pull yourself up out of the pit of dejection and failure, for His thoughts are power thoughts.

Chapter 7
Invisible Faith

When Moses came into contact with the supernatural, the course of his life was abruptly interrupted. His eyesight became clearer. He was a changed man. Before the incident he saw with his natural eye. He did things in his own power. He saw one of his people being brutally mistreated, and so he tried to work it out by his own insight or strength. He had not met the invisible God yet. He saw only the visible, tangible reality of life.

The morning he had an encounter with someone invisible put him in a new dimension. First of all an angel went and got inside a bush and started a fire in the midst of the bush. When Moses saw the flames of fire engulf the bush, but the bush remaining green, he said, "Something strange is going on. I must turn aside, change my course and check this out. Why is the bush not burnt?"

It was a test for Moses. If Moses had not turned aside and changed his natural habitual action, I wonder if God would have spoken to him. What if he would have ignored the supernatural? What would have happened? The scripture says, "And when the Lord saw that he turned aside to see, God called unto him out of the midst of the bush, and said, Moses, Moses. And he said, Here am I" (Exodus 3:4).

God did not speak until Moses made strides in the direction of the supernatural. He sought it out, made his way toward it; then God spoke. Moses stood and talked to a voice that was speaking from out of a bush. It sounds weird, crazy, and irrational, but he talked to a bush. Moses saw something other than the bush. He sensed the presence of God. There was a holy hush surrounding him. He saw the invisible God.

A conversation ensued that included the future of the children of Israel. God gave Moses the instructions telling him exactly what to do. When Moses doubted that the people would believe him, the Lord asked, "What is in thine hand?"

Moses answered, "A rod."

The Lord told him to throw it down. When Moses threw it down it became a serpent, and Moses ran quickly away from it. Remember, Moses could not see God at this point, only the serpent. He could hear God, but he could not see Him. When the Lord told Moses to stop running and go back and pick the snake up by the tail, notice that Moses obeyed Him.

Why did Moses obey? Would you obey a voice in the air and pick up a snake? Moses did, because he saw the invisible God by faith. "By faith he forsook Egypt, not fearing the wrath of the king: for he endured, as seeing him who is invisible" (Hebrews 11:27). Faith sees the invisible, believes the incredible, and receives the impossible.

You can obey God when you start seeing Him, even though you do not see Him with the natural eye. Seeing is more than seeing as we know it. It is looking beyond. In the city of Valladolid, the ancient capital of Spain, is a monument erected to commemorate the discoveries made by Christopher Columbus. The most noticeable feature of the monument is a lion with his paw raised as if to erase part of the words which had formed Spain's national motto: *Ne Plus Ultra* (Nothing Beyond).

For many hundreds of years the sailors who ventured forth into the Atlantic Ocean believed they had reached the boundaries of the earth. Europe, Asia and Africa lay behind them, and there was nothing before them as far as they knew, but the limitless expanse of the Atlantic Ocean. To them, the coast of Spain was the end, nothing beyond.

But when Christopher Columbus returned from his voyage in 1492 and reported discoveries of a vast continent and many islands, the motto was changed from *Ne Plus Ultra* to *Plus Ultra,* (More Beyond)!

Just as there was more beyond in the world, there is more beyond in the spirit. Seeing Him who is invisible enlarges your capacity of faith. Although He is invisible, it does not take away His power. He is all powerful, omnipresent and omnipotent! He cannot be seen, but He is there.

At one time a Christian from Jerusalem was greatly discouraged when making a missionary journey in Abyssinia. All seemed against him and he felt God had forsaken him. He found a cave and went into it, spending a long time in prayer, telling God how forsaken he was. It was very dark in the cave, but after he had remained in the dark for some time, his eyes became accustomed to it and he saw there a ferocious wild animal, a hyena and her cubs.

God had protected him, and the animals had made no move to touch him. God's hand at that very hour was with him even when he felt alone, and was keeping him from being torn to pieces, for there is no animal more ferocious than a hyena with her cubs. The invisible God was there, and he escaped unharmed. Oh, that we would open our eyes in the darkness and see the invisible God who is ever mindful of His children, keeping them from many unseen dangers and calamities.

The invisible must become greater than the visible. A little Chinese woman stood balancing herself on her tiny bound feet with the aid of a cane. She was listening to a missionary telling the story of Jesus to a group of women. "That is wonderful," she said to herself, "but the foreigner must be mistaken. I will ask the Chinese woman who is with the missionary if the story is true."

"Yes, it is true," said the Chinese woman in answer to her question, "and I will come and see you and tell you more."

The next day the Bible woman went to call on her new acquaintance. She spent an hour telling her of the Gospel story and about the one true God. Finally the old lady said she believed and great joy and peace came into her heart. A few nights later she had a strange dream. A great light fell across the floor of her room and the idols on the shelf began to move. Then a figure whom she took to be Jesus stood in the doorway, and all the idols climbed down from the shelf.

"Where are you going?" she asked them.

"When Jesus comes, we have to get out," they replied.

When the revelation of the power of Christ enters into your heart and the greatness of God sets up residence in your mind, then all the idols of doubt, fear, unbelief, and skepticism have to go. They cannot abide in the same house together. One or the other has to go. The thing we bow down to and believe in becomes an idol if it is not God. What rules us? What is the more powerful voice in our mind and hearts? Is faith in God our scepter, or is foolish doubt and fear?

Faith refuses facts. Reality says you are going to die. Faith says you are going to live. In April 1992, Jag Chatwraith was involved in a head-on automobile collision. When he was rushed to the hospital, he was in a coma. His brain was swollen and his face was pushed out of shape so much that the doctors said he would have to have massive plastic surgery. They also said he probably would not live, but if he did live he would be a vegetable. He would never walk, talk, or have understanding.

The church started praying, and the ministry went to be with him and his family at the hospital. The wife heard about the miracles of the ladies prayer group, so she asked them to come to the hospital and pray. There were seven ladies that gathered around Jag Chatwraith's bed at San Joaquin General Hospital. He was hooked up to several machines, and tubes were everywhere.

We began to pray quietly at first, and then with more intensity. Then we started taking authority over the spirit of death. We commanded the coma to loose its hold on him. Almost as soon as we started praying, bells started ringing and he started thrashing around on the bed, and the nurse came running to see what the commotion was about. We prayed almost an hour, and finally the nurse told us that the doctors needed to come in to do their rounds, and asked us kindly to come back another time. Before we left, we read Mark 11:22-24 to him, and we saw a big tear roll down his cheek.

We started praising the Lord for that miracle. We knew he had heard and understood the Word of God. We then asked him to squeeze our hand if he wanted to say "Praise the Lord," and he squeezed our hand. We knew then for sure that he would be alright.

I asked the nurse standing by Jag's bed, "Do you believe in miracles?"

She nodded her head yes and said, "Yes, miracles do happen sometime."

I told her, "I believe God did a miracle for Jag today. I believe he will walk again."

When we walked out of the intensive care unit, the hallway was lined with all the doctors and several of the nurses. They were all quiet in reverent silence just watching us. We could feel the presence of God lingering in those corridors. The invisible God was there in a powerful way!

It was May 27, 1992, while we were praying on KCJH radio station during the 10:00 a.m. prayer hour, that we received a phone call. It was a praise report from Jag himself. He said, "I was in a bad accident in a coma for twenty days. Doctors wanted to turn the machines off, because they said I would not live. Now they are calling me 'the walking miracle' at the three hospitals that I was in. God healed me and I am walking and talking, and I did not have to have plastic surgery."

We knew when it happened. We felt the invisible God walk in that hospital room and do the work. It did not happen immediately, but seven days to the day of that circle of prayer by those seven women around his bed, he opened his eyes and came out of the coma. God can do anything! Before He can do it, we must see Him who is invisible. We must believe when there is nothing there but God, for with God all things are possible.

When the angel appeared to Mary and told her that she was highly favored, and that she had been chosen to bring forth the Christ-child, Mary did not say, "This cannot be. You have got the wrong girl." She knew it was possible. She only asked how it would be done. The angel told her to fear not. "For with God nothing shall be impossible" (Luke 1:37).

The invisible God became visible for a short while by manifesting Himself in the flesh. John said,

In the beginning was the Word, and the Word was with God, and the Word was God. And the Word was made flesh, and dwelt among us, (and we beheld his glory, the glory as of the only begotten of the Father,) full of grace and truth (John 1:1,14).

If we could just see Him who is invisible, we would never be afraid again, although there are those who are afraid of the supernatural. People get comfortable with worry, doubt, fears, and morbid situations. They do not want their boat rocked or anything out of the ordinary to happen because they do not know how to handle it. They lose control, so they prefer to keep the normal or the status quo.

It is like the incident that happened in Spain. In Barcelona, a truck was rolling along carrying an empty coffin. A farmer who was hitchhiking thumbed a ride. He was bouncing along in the rear of the truck, which was open, when it started to rain. He examined the coffin, found it empty, and crawled inside to keep dry. There he fell asleep with the lid propped open just slightly.

Further on, two other hitchhikers got a ride on the truck. They were going along at a lively clip when the farmer inside the coffin pushed open the lid, stuck his head out, and observed, "Oh, it has stopped raining." The two other hitchhikers were so terrified that they leaped from the speeding truck and one was killed.

This is what happens in the spirit. The invisible God makes Himself known as He did to Moses, and some people run from it and commit spiritual suicide. They abort the higher purpose of God. Instead of talking to the bush, they scoff at it, deny it, or get as far away from it as possible. Moving in the spirit is bigger than them, so they are terrified of it. It is easier to just let things happen instead of using the shield of faith against the enemy's tactics. Faith in the invisible is what is needed in this generation. Too much emphasis is placed on the news coverage and the evident disaster. It is time to let God be God and to believe in the supernatural more than ever before! Do not run from it, but believe in it, for there is all power in the invisible God.

Chapter 8
Done Faith

Done faith knows it is done before it is done. When I was about ten years old, several warts came on my hand. There was an older deacon, Brother Hall, that was known to pray for warts and they would go away. One night my mother took me to him and said, "Brother Hall, Joy wants these warts to go off her hands." He looked at me and said, "Do you believe they will go away?" Innocently as a child, I nodded my head yes and felt inside of me that they had already started going away. He said, "Then they will go away after I pray." Sure enough! After he prayed and I believed, they disappeared.

Done faith speaks "it is done" when there is no sign. The Bible tells an interesting story about Elijah, a man who operated in the realm of done faith. When King Ahab made a grove for the promotion of idol worship, it provoked the Lord more than anything that all the other kings before Ahab had done.

Elijah sensed the Lord's anger and told Ahab, "As the Lord God of Israel liveth, before whom I stand, there shall not be dew nor rain these years, but according to my word" (I Kings 17:1). Notice, he did not say according to the word of the Lord; he said according to *my* word. I do not find where God told him to go tell Ahab this dire news either. He just spoke it, because he walked close to the invisible God and had an understanding of His power.

After he spoke the news, then the Lord spoke to him and told him to go hide by the brook Cherith. There the Lord fed Elijah by sending meat and bread held in the mouth of the ravens, which they deposited in Elijah's lap. Finally after several miracles and three years later, the word of the Lord came to Elijah, "...saying, Go, shew thyself unto Ahab; and I will send rain upon the earth" (I Kings 18:1). God had not forgotten what his prophet, Elijah, had spoken three years before.

Elijah challenged Ahab with a contest between the prophets of Baal and the one true God. Then all of Israel met at Mount Carmel. When they all arrived at the scene of the contest, Elijah asked them a pertinent question, "How long halt ye between two opinions? if the Lord be God, follow him: but if Baal, then follow him. And the people answered him not a word" (I Kings 18:21).

There was not one ounce of doubt in Elijah's mind who was God, but there was in the minds of the people. So the big contest began. When Baal could not perform, Elijah took charge again, and there was a mighty manifestation of the power of God as the fire rained from heaven and licked up stones, water, and the altar--so much that the people fell on their faces and cried, "The Lord He is God!"

Notice what Elijah did after the victory. He slew the propagators of doubt and announced to Ahab, "Get thee up, eat and drink; for there is a sound of abundance of rain" (I Kings 18:41). He said it before it was done. All he had to go on was the word of the Lord. There was not a drop of rain to encourage him. The dust swirled up in his nostrils, and the earth lay parched around him as if to mock his faith.

What did he do then? He went up to pray. He did not pray a lofty prayer, but a humble one. Ahab went up to eat and drink, but Elijah, who walked in a different realm than Ahab, cast himself on the ground prostrate before the invisible God. He prayed not once, but as many times as it took to get a sign from God. He did not need the rain, only a sign. His servant kept telling him there was nothing every time he would send him to look, so Elijah just kept praying.

Finally on the seventh time the servant came to him and said,

Behold, there ariseth a little cloud out of the sea, like a man's hand. And he said, Go up, say unto Ahab, Prepare thy chariot, and get thee down, that the rain stop thee not. And it came to pass in the mean while, that the heaven was black with clouds and wind, and there was a great rain (I Kings 18:44-45).

The whole point is this: Elijah called it done before it was done. He spoke it first, and then prayed it into existence. He did not worry that it would not come to pass. He knew that it would come to pass, but he also knew that he needed to pray until it did. We can speak until we are blue in the face, but if we do not pray, it will not happen. Prayer is the power line between God and man.

This kind of authority was not just relegated to Elijah. Jesus talked about the authority of the church in the book of Matthew when Peter answered Jesus and said,

> ...Thou art the Christ, the Son of the living God. And Jesus answered and said unto him, Blessed art thou, Simon Barjona for flesh and blood hath not revealed it unto thee, but my Father which is in heaven. And I say also unto thee, That thou art Peter, and upon this rock I will build my church; and the gates of hell shall not prevail against it. And I will give unto thee the keys of the kingdom of heaven: and whatsoever thou shalt bind on earth shall be bound in heaven: and whatsoever thou shalt loose on earth shall be loosed in heaven (Matthew 16:16-19).

The church can call it as done, and heaven will back them up. What is the church? It is not a building, it is flesh and blood. It is anyone that bears the name of Jesus and accepts and embraces His doctrine. Men, women, boys, and girls have the distinct privilege to enter into this realm of faith, if they stay close to Jesus, for that is where the power is.

When the fate of our nation was hanging precariously in the balances, and General Lee and his army had surged forward to the city of Gettysburg where the fateful, decisive battle of the Civil War was in the making, the question was asked President Lincoln how he could be so calm and self-assured. His serenity was reassuring to his generals, but puzzling.

When they inquired, "How can you be so self-possessed in this hour of the nation's mortal peril and darkness?", Lincoln said, "I spent last night in prayer before the Lord. He has given to me the assurance that our cause will triumph and that the nation will be preserved!"

He lived to see that prophecy come to pass. He spoke it before it was done. He could only have that kind of faith and assurance because he had spent all night in the presence of the great invisible God. Doubt will rule your life if you do not pray every day and stay in contact with power, which is God.

In another story, Elisha spoke a word before it was done, and it fell on an unbeliever's ear. Did the unbeliever's doubt affect the validity of what was spoken by the prophet? No! It came to pass anyway, but the doubter did not participate in the blessing associated with it. Elisha said,

Thus saith the Lord, Tomorrow about this time shall a measure of fine flour be sold for a shekel, and two measures of barley for a shekel, in the gate of Samaria. Then a lord on whose hand the king leaned answered the man of God, and said, Behold, if the Lord would make windows in heaven, might this thing be? (II Kings 7:1-2).

It was as good as done even when Elisha spoke it, but the man close to the king did not believe in "done faith."

He sarcastically tried to throw water on the word of Elisha, but Elisha said to him, "...Behold, thou shalt see it with thine eyes, but shalt not eat thereof" (II Kings 7:2). Be careful of what you say. The word of the Lord shall come to pass, but if you want to partake of it, you better believe it as done.

What happened to the unbelieving man?

And it came to pass as the man of God had spoken to the king, saying, Two measures of barley for a shekel, and a measure of fine flour for a shekel, shall be tomorrow about this time in the gate of Samaria: And that lord answered the man of God, and said, Now, behold, if the Lord should make windows in heaven, might such a thing be? And he said, Behold, thou shalt see it with thine eyes, but shalt not eat thereof. And so it fell out unto him: for the people trode upon him in the gate, and he died (II Kings 7:18-20).

Be careful of those "ifs." Adam and Eve listened to the doubting ifs and died. This man injected *if* into his thinking and he died. Do not question God's word. If he said it, there are no ifs! The devil always puts question marks where God puts a period. He used this tactic when tempting Jesus. "If thou be the Son of God" was the way he approached Him. Jesus did not argue; He just said, "It is written," for that was the only thing that worked on the devil.

While speaking and ministering in a church in Tennessee in April 1992, the pastor's wife shared with me the need of one of the women in their congregation. At the end of my message, I asked the woman to come up front for prayer. The need sounded impossible, but with God all things are possible to him that believeth. The need was this: the husband, wife and family were going to lose their house by May 1 if they did not come up with $30,000 by that time.

I looked her straight in the eye and asked her if there was any way possible for them to get the money. She said, "We have tried everything, and in three weeks we are going to lose it because the state is going to put it up for auction. There is no way possible for us to get $30,000."

I asked her, "Have you tried working with the banks? Surely they would help you."

She answered, "We have gone to all the banks, and no one can help us under the circumstances."

I then talked to her and the congregation and asked them to raise their hands if they believed that God would help this family to not lose their house. About ninety percent of them raised their hands. We prayed together a simple prayer, but one with authority. We bound every spirit of doubt that would exalt itself above the knowledge of God, and asked God to rebuke the devourer. We then prayed the scripture in Ephesians 3:20, "Now unto him that is able to do exceeding abundantly above all that we ask or think, according to the power that worketh in us."

When we finished praying we quoted Philippians 4:19, "But my God shall supply all your need according to his riches in glory by Jesus Christ."

I then told the lady, "You leave no stone unturned. You do everything that you can do and God will do the rest. The miracle is done if you will believe."

The first week of May, I received a card from the pastor's wife postmarked April 30. These were her words:

Just wanted to tell you of another miracle. The girl we prayed for that was losing her home--it has been taken care of through His miracle- working power, plus $3,000 extra for them! Praise the Lord! It was up to be auctioned off May 1; God answered April 29th.

It was done when we prayed. Not only done, but God did exceeding abundantly above what we prayed for. He gave them an extra $3000.00 we did not pray for. He always does all things well. If we will just believe, it is done. We cannot excuse our failure to believe, only humbly repent and ask God to increase our faith. We must not reason, debate or question God's word. The Word is the Word--final and direct--meaning exactly what it says. It says, "Therefore I say unto you, What things soever ye desire, when ye pray, believe that ye receive them, and ye shall have them" (Mark 11:24). It also says, "And *all* things, whatsoever ye shall ask in prayer, believing, ye shall receive" (Matthew 21:22).

Many times when we quote the above scripture found in Ephesians 3:20, we just flip it off not registering the true meaning into our subconscious mind. We read, but we do not comprehend. The scripture is actually saying this: God is able to do exceeding or extraordinary, more than sufficient, abundantly, amply, profuse, plenty, above, surpassing, beyond, more than, beyond all doubt--He can do so much farther above what even our subconscious mind or conscious mind can conceive. The magnificent mind that He put within us is puny compared with His power. He is God and nothing is impossible for Him, if we can just believe!

Chapter 9

Mind Faith

No one knows exactly what the mind is. It has tremendous power, but it cannot be seen, felt, weighed, or surgically dissected. It is affected by damage done to the brain, and is related to intelligence and personality. The mind influences how each of us lives and thinks. It has been proven that the mind can be controlled by others, ourselves, and molded by God. In Gary Collin's book *Your Magnificent Mind* he states,

> The Mind refers to the total of all our mental activities---including thinking, learning, problem-solving, willing, perceiving, concentrating, remembering, attending, and experiencing thoughts and emotions.

What does the mind have to do with faith? Jesus connects the two together. He is speaking to them of His ability to provide their needs for them such as food, clothing, and drink, then makes a statement about them. "O ye of little faith" (Luke 12:28). The very next scripture says,

And seek not ye what ye shall eat, or what ye shall drink, neither be ye of doubtful mind. For all these things do the nations of the world seek after: and your Father knoweth that ye have need of these things, But rather seek ye the kingdom of God; and all these things shall be added unto you (Luke 12:29-31).

Little faith produces a doubtful mind. There is war in the mind every day. Paul writes,

But I see another law in my members, warring against the law of my *mind,* and bringing me into captivity to the law of sin which is in my members...I thank God through Jesus Christ our Lord, So then with the *mind* I myself serve the law of God; but with the flesh the law of sin (Romans 7:23,25).

The mind has power. It is the crowning creation of God Almighty. The mind of man is magnificent, but can be abused or used for a noble cause. The choice is determined by what is fed into the mind. The power of the mind was recognized by God when He came down to see the city and the tower which the children of men builded. "And the Lord said, Behold, the people is one, and they have all one language; and this they begin to do: and now nothing will be restrained from them, which they have imagined to do" (Genesis 11:6). It was in their mind to build a tower of Babel, and they would have done so if the Lord had not thwarted their plans. Nothing is impossible to the human mind, God says, when there is faith involved.

Ships, electricity, radar, automobiles, atomic power have all been the result of thought.

Since the mind has such power it needs to be controlled, and it is possible to do so. Peter instructs each of us to "...gird up the loins of your mind, be sober, and hope to the end..." (I Peter 1:13). *Gird* means to tighten or constrict, to not just hang loose, but to control. He said control the loins of the mind. Loins are part of the reproductive organs. Genesis 35:11 shows this: "And God said unto him, I am God Almighty: be fruitful and multiply; a nation and a company of nations shall be of thee, and kings shall come out of thy loins."

Whatever thoughts and attitudes are conceived in the mind will multiply whether they be of evil or of good. Kings will come forth--kings that will rule. Kings such as bitterness, fear, jealousy, worldliness and doubt, or on the other hand, kings of faith, love, peace, joy, power, and a sound mind.

The mind is fertile. It conceives and then it gives birth. It is constantly absorbing information. The information absorbed will produce corresponding products. It is possible to keep the mind in positive gear at all times by the renewing of it. You can change! The negative world system does not have to dominate you. "And be not conformed to this world: but be ye transformed by the renewing of your mind, that ye may prove what is that good, and acceptable, and perfect, will of God" (Romans 12:2).

The mind of Christ was ever active towards helping those that needed to be helped. His actions were deliberate, positive, and full of faith. To every person with whom He came in contact that needed a miracle, He talked about faith. The element of faith was never separated from Him. It was an integral part of His system. When Paul writes to the Philippians he tells them to have the *mind* of Christ. When he says, "Let this mind be in you, which was also in Christ Jesus" (Philippians 2:5), he is talking about humility and submission.

If Jesus had the attitude of a servant, was obedient to the cross and the purpose of heaven, so should His followers be to the higher purpose. It is impossible to do this without faith. Faith in God must be an integral part of the mind in order to operate in the realm Jesus operated.

It is possible to have a blinded mind and not be able to see the purpose of Christ and be sensitive to His perfect plan. The blinded mind is referred to in II Corinthians 3:14: "But their minds were blinded." Paul talks about there being enemies in the mind, (Colossians 1:21). Not enemies *of* the mind, but enemies *in* the mind. That means they were resident; they lived there trying to blind them to the will of God. Anything that exalts itself against the knowledge of God is an enemy in the mind. Those enemies must be dealt with and kicked out--not subdued, but brought into captivity and then thrown out. "Casting down imaginations, and every high thing that exalteth itself against the knowledge of God, and bringing into captivity every thought to the obedience of Christ" (II Corinthians 10:5).

It is important to not be shaken in your mind. "That ye be not soon shaken in mind, or be troubled..." (II

Thessalonians 2:2). Guard the mind, for that is where it all happens. Nothing is put into action except the mind dictate it first. Guard against having a doubting, blinded mind which is built on wrong thoughts. When the storm comes, the enemies of deceit will have eaten away at the very foundation of faith and truth causing a flood of the enemy's suggestion to destroy everything.

You can open up your mind to the lies of Satan and he can make you believe something that is not true. Paul talks about this in II Corinthians 4:4: "In whom the god of this world hath blinded the minds of them which believe not..." It is imperative to have faith, lest Satan, the god of this world system, will blind the mind. But Paul gives hope. "For who hath known the *mind* of the Lord, that he may instruct him? But we have the *mind* of Christ" (I Corinthians 1:16).

God's power is more powerful than the god of this world. Put your faith in God and you will win. "That your faith should not stand in the wisdom of men, but in the power of God, Howbeit we speak wisdom among them that are perfect: yet not the wisdom of this world, not of the princes of this world, that come to nought" (I Corinthians 2:5-6). All wisdom is going to come to nought, except the wisdom of God. Put your investment in God's word; that is where the reward is.

There was once a man that lived in the country of the Gadarenes, near the sea of Galilee. That man was driven by spirits so much that he could not keep his clothes on, so they chained him to the tombstones in the cemetery.

When a certain spirit came upon him, he would break the chains, and terror would reign in the nearby community.

One day Jesus walked near the naked man, and the spirits inside of him cried for Jesus to not torment them. When Jesus spoke, He commanded the unclean spirits to come out of him. Later when news reached the people of the village, they went out to see for themselves what had happened. "Then they went out to see what was done; and came to Jesus, and found the man, out of whom the devils were departed, sitting at the feet of Jesus, clothed, and in his *right mind*" (Luke 8:35).

Attitudes and spirits that are not rooted in the wisdom of God always torment and take away the rightness of the mind. When Jesus dealt with the problem of the Gadarene, his right mind was restored to him. Jesus gives love, power, and sound minds (II Timothy 1:7); whereas the devil gives fear, confusion, and depression. It is essential to build a mind of faith. Just as Jesus told His followers that they must love Him with all their heart, soul, mind, and strength (Mark 12:30), even so, it is important to let faith have its perfect work in the mind. Feed the mind with things that build, strengthen, and produce things that will glorify God. Do not leave the mind open for spirits that attack faith, but be on guard to constantly build up the holy faith given by God. You are spirit dwelling in a fleshly body. It is not the body that determines who you are, it is the mind. If you constantly feed into your mind phrases such as, "You can't trust anyone," or "People are just out to get what they can out of you," or "Nobody loves me," or "I just feel sick all the time," then you are feeding the wrong kind of thoughts that will eventually manifest themselves. "For as he thinketh in his heart, so is he" (Proverbs 23:7).

If you can believe in your mind that God has already taken care of a problem, it is as good as done. He said,

Verily, I say unto you, If ye have faith, and doubt not, ye shall not only do this which is done to the fig tree, but also if ye shall say unto this mountain, Be thou removed, and be thou cast into the sea; it shall be done. And all things, whatsoever ye shall ask in prayer, believing, ye shall receive (Matthew 21:21-22).

A poet and an artist were once examining a painting by a famous artist depicting the healing of the two blind men of Jericho. The artist asked, "What seems to you the most remarkable thing in this painting?" The poet replied, "Everything in the painting is excellently portrayed--the form of Christ, the grouping of the individuals, the expression of the faces of the leading characters."

The artist seemed to find the most significant feature elsewhere. He said to his friend, pointing to the steps of a house in the corner of the picture, "Do you see that discarded cane lying there?"

"Yes, but what does it signify?" asked the other.

The artist answered, "On those steps the blind man sat with the cane in his hand, but when he heard Christ had come he was so sure that he would be healed that he let his cane lie there, since he would need it no more, and hastened to the Lord as if he could already see."

That is faith! Throwing away the canes and crutches of man's wisdom and doubt. Throwing caution to the wind, and believing it is done before it is done. Faith always takes the first step forward. It is a spiritual foresight, which peers far beyond the physical eye's vision. It is a courier which leads the way, opens the closed door, and sees beyond the obstacles.

When a woman of Canaan came to Jesus and cried to him for help, the disciples decided she was a nuisance and wanted to get rid of her. But she did not leave; she fell down before the Lord and worshipped Him. Jesus discouraged her and told her that He was only helping the Jews at that particular time. She said, "Truth, Lord; yet the dogs eat of the crumbs which fall from their masters' table" (Matthew 15:27).

When Jesus saw her persistent faith, He said, "O woman, great is thy faith: be it unto thee even as thou wilt. And her daughter was made whole from that very hour" (Matthew 15:28). It was not protocol, traditional, or expected by the religious body, but she expected it and received what she believed was already done. Her mind was made up before she went to Jesus. That is how she could be so persistent and not intimidated by what tradition dictated. Jesus did not let her down because He always honors faith! When faith is present, He always performs.

If Jesus instructed His followers to not be of a doubtful mind, how do you obey this commandment?

Psychologists say that 10,000 thoughts go through the human mind in one day. That is over 3,500,000 a year. According to the American Medical Association, sitting up in bed increases your energy requirements ten percent; standing nearly doubles it; chopping wood causes your needs to shoot up nearly eight times. The interesting thing is, heavy thinking requires hardly any energy at all.

My questions are, What do you think about all day long? Do you think of the wrong someone did you, or the trial of yesterday? Is your mind on other people's faults, or is it filled with fear and depression? What do you extend your thinking ability towards? How many hours a day do you meditate and think on the word of God? What demands attention in your mind? Do you hear something that is tinged with doubt and dwell on it, or worse, even believe it?

Napoleon often told the story that while visiting a province he came on an old soldier with one arm severed, who was dressed in full uniform. On his uniform he displayed the Legion of Honor award. Napoleon asked him where he had lost his arm, and the soldier told him he lost it at Austerlitz.

"You must be," the emperor said, "the kind of man who regrets he did not lose both arms for his country."

"What then would have been my reward?" asked the one-armed man.

"Then," Napoleon replied, "I would have awarded you a double Legion of Honor." With that the proud old fighter drew his sword and immediately cut off his other arm.

The story was circulated for years. Finally, one day someone asked, "How?"

Often people accept half-truths just because they are the general belief. The only truth to believe is the word of God. Does it not say in I Peter 2:24 that by His stripes we were healed already, and in James 5:16 that the prayer of faith *shall,* not *maybe,* but *shall* save the sick, and the Lord *shall* raise him up? Does it not say in Matthew 9:29 that according to your faith be it unto you? What is our mind filled with--faith, doubt, or traditional beliefs that float around among us because they are comfortable to believe in, and it has always been that way? What will we choose to fill our minds with--fictional novels, shady magazines, faithless talk, circumstances, or God's Word?

You only have one mind and you must use it for good. You are spirit dwelling within a fleshly body, but that body is controlled by the conscious and subconscious mind. Man has been given a seed of faith that he uses every day unconsciously. He has faith that when he eats, the food consumed will be turned into blood, cells, and other needful things for the body. He has faith to build, conquer, invent, and think.

When it looked like Great Britain had lost World War II, it was then that Winston Churchill made the memorable speech:

We shall defend our island whatever the cost may be; we shall fight on the beaches; we shall fight in the fields; we shall fight in the streets; and we shall fight in the hills. We shall never surrender and if this island were subjugated and starving, our empire on the seas would carry on the struggle until in God's good time the New World with all its power and might steps forth to the rescue and liberation of the old.

This was positive faith believing in a cause. This winning attitude is important and needful and must be applied in a Christian's life against the enemy of your soul, but there is a higher level of faith in God. It is more than the power of the mind that God has given to mankind. It is not believing in our power, but it is believing in His power. As we decrease in our own reasoning and trying to figure things out, He increases in us. Faith washes away our questions, doubts, and fears. "For God hath not given us the spirit of fear; but of power, and of love, and of a sound mind" (II Timothy 1:7).

It is His word and spirit in us. Paul wrote, "For this cause also thank we God without ceasing, because when ye received the word of God which ye heard of us, ye received it not as the word of men, but as it is in truth, the word of God, which effectually worketh also in you *that believe*" (I Thessalonians 2:13).

The Word works if we believe in our minds.

Chapter 10
Word Faith

There is nothing more powerful than the word of God, for the word of God *is* God. "In the beginning was the Word, and the Word was with God and the Word was God" (John 1:1). "Through faith we understand that the worlds were framed by the word of God, so that things which are seen were not made of things which do appear" (Hebrews 11:3).

"For the word of God is quick, and powerful, and sharper than any twoedged sword, piercing even to the dividing asunder of soul and spirit, and of the joints and marrow, and is a discerner of the thoughts and intents of the heart" (Hebrews 4:12). The word of God is effective any way you use it. There is no wasted motion. It is electrifying power in action.

Let the church become more aware of the power of the word of God. The Bible is without question the inspired word of God, even though there are those who are ignorant enough to question it. When Voltaire, the noted 18th century French philosopher, said that it took centuries to build up Christianity, but that he would show how one Frenchman could destroy it within fifty years, he made a bold, but regrettable statement. After having tried to squelch the truth of Jesus Christ during his lifetime, just before his death he swore, "I wish I had never been born."

Napoleon said, "A man is not a man without God. I saw men without God in the reign of terror in 1793. One does not govern such men; he shoots them down." That is a strong statement, but what he was saying was that men who do not know God have no conscience and they become as animals. It is best to believe and grow into Christlikeness, instead of not believing and debase into corruptness.

Mary, the mother of Jesus, believed. After the angel made the profound statement, "For with God nothing shall be impossible" (Luke 1:37), Mary confessed her faith. "And Mary said, Behold, the handmaid of the Lord; be it unto me according to thy word" (Luke 1:38). The angel being on a mission from God was giving Mary the word of God, and Mary chose to believe.

The word always works! The people were astonished many times by the power of the spoken word of Jesus. When Jesus rebuked a demon, "...they were all amazed, and spake among themselves, saying, What a *word* is this! for with authority and power he commandeth the unclean spirits, and they come out" (Luke 4:38). "When the even was come, they brought unto him many that were possessed with devils: and he cast out the spirits with his *word,* and healed all that were sick" (Matthew 8:16).

The confidence of many was placed in the power of Jesus. When a centurion went to Jesus and asked Him to heal his servant, he showed faith by expressing that Jesus did not need to come in person. He said, "...say in a word, and my servant shall be healed" (Luke 7:7). When Jesus heard him speak about the authority he had and how he believed Jesus had authority, "Jesus...marvelled at him, and turned him about, and said unto the people that followed him, I say unto you, I have not found so great faith, no not in Israel" (Luke 7:9). When they returned to the house, the servant was healed. Jesus just sent His *word*. That is all that was needed.

Over 100 years ago, William Ramsay, a young English scholar, went to Asia Minor with the expressed purpose of proving that the history given by Luke in his gospel and in the Acts was inaccurate. His professors had taught over and over that Luke could not possibly be right.

He began to dig in the ancient ruins of Greece and Asia Minor, testing for ancient terms, boundaries, and other items which would be a dead giveaway if a writer had been inventing this history at a later date as claimed. To his amazement, he found that the New Testament scriptures were accurate to the tiniest detail. So convincing was the evidence that Ramsay himself became a disciple of Christ and a great biblical scholar. Sir William Ramsay's books are still considered as being a classic as far as the history of the New Testament is concerned.

The Bible is true. It is not only for one generation, but it is for every generation. It is "Jesus Christ the same yesterday, today, and forever" (Hebrews 13:8). He still heals, answers prayer, delivers, and sets the captive free.

He has not changed; only sophisticated mankind has changed. When there is faith anything is possible.

Word faith is powerful. When Peter had fished all night and the fish barrels were empty, he and his crew were very discouraged. Along comes the Word made flesh: Jesus. Jesus told Peter the secret to getting the fish was to let the net down on the right side. Peter said, "Master, we have toiled all the night, and have taken nothing: nevertheless at thy *word* I will let down the net" (Luke 5:5). When they followed the words of Jesus, the ingathering of fish was so great that the net broke. They hollered to their partners in other ships and said, "Come and help us." They filled both ships and they both began to sink. Then Peter repented and asked the Lord to forgive him for doubting, for they were astonished about the great draught of fishes they had taken.

What changed? Nothing, except now the Word entered into the picture. The Word changed everything. There is more power in the Word than a trillion sticks of dynamite. The word of God made the oceans, birds, animals, and firmament. The word is God. It is highly exalted even above the powerful name. David pens these words: "I will worship toward thy holy temple, and praise thy name for thy lovingkindness and for thy truth: for thou hast magnified thy word above all thy name" (Psalm 138:2).

When Hezekiah became king of Judah, the king of Assyria sent messengers to his kingdom and tried to convince the people not to listen to Hezekiah because he was telling them to trust in the Lord. The messengers were questioning everything Hezekiah had said. They said,

"Let not Hezekiah deceive you. Neither let Hezekiah make you trust in the Lord, for Hezekiah will persuade you and say, The Lord will deliver us."

When word got back to King Hezekiah what was being said, he rent his clothes, fell on his face and called on the Lord. The prophet Isaiah got wind of all this and sent a word to King Hezekiah. "Thus saith the Lord, Be not afraid of the words which thou hast heard, with which the servant of the king of Assyria have blasphemed me. Behold, I will send a blast upon him, and he shall hear a rumour, and shall return to his own land; and I will cause him to fall by the sword in his own land" (II Kings 19:6-7).

Hezekiah kept praying even after this word from the Lord because he had received a letter from the king of Assyria saying to him, "...Let not thy God in whom thou trustest deceive thee..." (II Kings 19:10). He went into the house of the Lord and spread the letter out and began to magnify God and ended up by asking, "Now therefore, O Lord our God, I beseech thee, save us out of his hand, that all the kingdoms of the earth may know that thou art the Lord God, even thou only" (II Kings 19:19). The Lord answered again through Isaiah and said, "Thy prayer I have heard and I will defend this city."

God always gets the last word. He will not be mocked forever. He is with those that put their faith in His word. Sure enough, as He spoke the first time and then the second time, His word came to pass. He sent one angel and smote the camp of the Assyrians. In the morning they were all dead corpses. One angel killed 145,000 men. God has more power than the whole earth. It is best not to challenge God. And yes, just as He had spoken the king of Assyria was killed in his own land, by his own sons, with the sword.

God's word always comes to pass. We can believe it, question it, or debate it, but it will never change. It is truth, every word of it, and man's opinion is worthless if it is not in accord with it. His word shall always come to pass. Sometimes you have to wait on the Lord, but that does not mean God is not answering. He moves at His own speed. Remember: impatience is not faith.

When Solomon stood before the congregation of the children of Israel he blessed them saying, "Blessed be the Lord, that hath given rest unto his people Israel, according to all that he promised: there hath *not failed one word of all his good promise, which he promised by the hand of Moses his servant*" (I Kings 8:56). Jesus never fails. He is faithful to what He promises in His Word.

The word cannot work properly, though, if we do not mix faith with it. There were those who did not enter into the rest because they did not believe. We were warned to believe, lest we lose out on all the promises. "For unto us was the gospel preached, as well as unto them: but the word preached did not profit them, not being *mixed with faith* in them that heard it" (Hebrews 4:2).

Chapter 11
Name Faith

There was a young lad that knew the power of the name. When David went to the camp to take his brothers an ephah of parched corn and ten loaves of bread, he entered a camp of fear. David had a different spirit. They were all trembling, but David asked, "...who is this uncircumcised Philistine, that he should defy the armies of the living God?" (I Samuel 17:26). He did not even acknowledge that he was a giant. He put more emphasis on his God than he did the enemy.

Finally when word circulated among the camp and eventually reached the ears of King Saul, David was sent for by the king. After discussing the matter of the challenge between Goliath and the army of Israel, it was agreed that David could go fight. Can you imagine the audacity of a king letting a young teenage boy go fight, while seasoned warriors hid behind rocks? It was absurd, crazy, and highly unusual. It had to be desperation and fear that dictated King Saul's decision, but not that alone. The king sensed an element of faith in David that was lacking in everyone else. He was still sensitive enough to know that when faith was present miracles could happen.

David was totally alone when he ran down that mountain towards Goliath. He had no armor bearer, and he wore no armor. You do not need fleshly crutches when God is involved. He does not need man's helps to do a miracle, only his faith, and that is what David possessed. When he got near Goliath and heard the ranting and ravings of the Philistine about all he was going to do to him and the army of Israel, David did not run back with fear. He kept going forward saying these powerful words:

> Thou comest to me with a sword, and with a spear, and with a shield; but I come to thee in the name of the Lord of hosts, the God of the armies of Israel, whom thou hast defied. This day will the Lord deliver thee into mine hand; and I will smite thee, and take thine head from thee; and I will give the carcasses of the host of the Philistines this day unto the fowls of the air, and to the wild beasts of the earth; that all the earth may know that there is a God in Israel. And all this assembly shall know that the Lord saveth not with sword and spear: for the battle is the Lord's and he will give you into our hands (I Samuel 17:45-47).

David spoke it before it was done. He put all the glory on the Lord and went in his power. It all happened just as he had spoken. God avenged Israel through his servant David whose faith was stronger in his God than in the circumstances. This is name faith: coming against circumstances with the powerful name of the Lord.

When Peter and John went up together into the temple at the hour of prayer, there was a lame man that sat nearby at the gate Beautiful. When he saw them going towards the temple he asked them for alms. Peter told him they did not have any money, but they had something more powerful than money. He said, "...In the name of Jesus Christ of Nazareth rise up and walk. And he took him by the right hand, and lifted him up: and immediately his feet and ankle bones received strength" (Acts 3:6-7).

When the people saw the familiar lame beggar up walking, leaping, and praising God, they wanted to know what had happened. Peter told them the reason for it all. "And his *name* through faith in his name hath made this man strong, whom ye see and know; yea, the faith which is by him hath given him this perfect soundness in the presence of you all" (Acts 3:16).

The man had the faith, but without the power of the name there would have been no miracle. Faith in something itself is not enough. There must be faith in the name of Jesus, for at the name of Jesus every knee is going to bow. It is a name to be revered, for it is the most powerful name on earth, and by it all men are saved and healed.

"Neither is there salvation in any other: for there is none other name under heaven given among men, whereby we must be saved" (Acts 4:12).

"And these signs shall follow them that believe; *In my name* shall they cast out devils; they shall speak with new tongues; they shall lay hands on the sick, and they shall recover" (Mark 16:17-18).

When the name of Jesus is evoked over a situation, it sets in motion catalytic movements, for His name is "Far above all principality, and power, and might, and dominion, and every name that is named, not only in this world, but also in that which is to come" (Ephesians 1:21).

Jesus is highly exalted, so high that every power is under His dominion. "At the name of Jesus every knee should bow, of things in heaven, and things in earth, and things under the earth" (Philippians 2:10). Did you read what was just quoted? The name has power over all inhabitants of the earth, heaven, and of hell. It is the only name that makes the devils tremble. They know there is only one God and they know His name is Jesus. "Thou believest that there is one God; thou doest well: the devils also believe, and tremble" (James 2:19).

The trembling devils--what a blessed sight! The demons are under the dominion of the name of Jesus. They have to let go of whatever they have hold when that name is applied with authority. They become very fearful when another one of God's children gets the revelation of the power of the name. As long as a Christian is passive with the name, they do not have to worry so much, but let Him get hold of the name and they break out in a cold sweat and have to flee for their lives. When Jesus sent the seventy people out to do His work throughout the villages, they came back excited at the end of their journey. They said, "...Lord, even the devils are subject unto us through *thy name*" (Luke 10:17).

One normal day a pretty young mother in a normal neighborhood answered a knock at her door, thinking it was the neighbor. It was not the neighbor; it was a masked man who pushed his way inside her home. Fear immediately gripped her and he tried to force her to go to the back side of the house away from her baby. He threatened to kill her, and stood but a foot away from her holding a revolver to her head.

When he told her to take her baby to the other side of the house, she refused his command. The girl and man just stared at one another, when suddenly she realized for the first time in her life that she was a child of the King of kings. And being His child she had more power than the man she faced. She started rebuking him in the name of Jesus.

The attacker showed a brief moment of uncertainty, then she noticed doubt and fear comes into his eyes. Looking oddly about the room he became more and more uneasy with his situation. Then suddenly he asked her, "Lady, do you have a back door? I've got the wrong house."

Who knows what really happened. Maybe he saw angels come into the room. Maybe the presence of God was so strong that the evil spirit within him quailed under the influence. The important thing was, the devil trembled at the name of Jesus, and he ran for his life.

We received a missionary report one time from Africa. The soldiers of the country walked boldly into a church service that was in progress and demanded the benches and everything in the building. The missionary stood up to them and told them no, they had worked hard to prepare everything for the Lord's work. While all this was going on, the missionary's wife was praying and repeating over and over, "In Jesus' name. In Jesus' name."

The soldiers said, "We're going to shoot you," but she just kept on praying. One of the soldiers shot and the bullet went into the floor, and then another one shot and his bullet went into the wall. Suddenly one grabbed the other and said, "Let's get out of here." These were trained soldiers. I wonder, did an angel jerk the guns when they fired them and make the shots go astray? Did God allow them to see the angels in that little humble church building? What made them turn around and run and give up so easily? It was the power of the name of Jesus!

In fact it is so powerful that Paul instructed the Colossians to use it in every circumstance. "And whatsoever ye do in word or deed, do *all* in the *name of Jesus...*" (Colossians 3:17). We treat the name of Jesus too casually, or ignore it too much. The name of Jesus should be held in awe, and become part of our very concepts, ideas, and practices. Christians are not powerless, although they act like they are sometimes. It is time to think on the name, and become acquainted with the God who bears the name, so we can utilize it more instead of living in the molygrubs so often.

The Lord promises protection to them that know His name. "Because he hath set his love upon me, therefore will I deliver him: I will set him on high, because he hath *known my name.* He shall call upon me, and I will answer him: I will be with him in trouble; I will deliver him, and honor him" (Psalm 91:14-15). The whole earth needs to know He can deliver out of any hand. "That they may know from the rising of the sun, and from the west, that there is none beside me, I am the Lord, and there is none else" (Isaiah 45:6).

John tells us in Revelation, "And there shall be no more curse: but the throne of God and of the Lamb shall be in it; and his servants shall serve him; And they shall see his face: and *his name shall be in their foreheads"* (Revelation 22:3-4). What is going to put the name of Jesus on the foreheads? Will it be marked by an angel? Or could it be that as the person thinks on the name so often, that it naturally appears showing the thought pattern of the individual? The name will be there and it will be an identification mark, but the name cannot be there if the individual does not know or revere the name.

The church needs a new revelation of the power of the name. Knowing about the name is not enough; the name must be thought upon, because a name represents a person. A name tells everything about someone. Malachi wrote, "Then they that feared the Lord spake often one to another: and the Lord hearkened, and heard it, and a book of remembrance was written before him for them that feared the Lord, and that thought upon his name" (Malachi 3:16).

There was once a saying that was quite popular: Hitch your wagon to a star. Upon reading this verse that quote came to my mind, only in a different sense: Hitch your thoughts to the bright and morning Star. If you want to win you must think upon the name, because you are what you think about all day long. You can think about the problems, or you can think about Jesus who can solve the problems. The next chapter will discuss the second meaning of this verse in Malachi.

Chapter 12
Saith Faith

Notice in a portion of the verse in Malachi 3:16 that they not only thought upon the name, but they spoke often one to another. You speak only what is computed into your brain. The whole verse is about fearing the Lord and thinking upon His name, so it is evident what their conversation was about. It centered around the name and the power of the name. The Word was rich to them, not something to be endured, but they ate it as a child would eat cotton candy. It was something to be desired. It was a treat, not only for special occasions, but every day the name was like honey or chocolate. It was never stale, boring, or musty; it quivered with delight on the tips of their tongues.

You get what you say! Be careful what you say, for it shall come to pass. Words never die; they are forever floating in the universe. Scientists tell us that the sound waves set in motion by our voices go upon an endless journey through space, and that, had we instruments delicate enough, and the power to take our stand upon some planet years afterwards, we might find them again and recreate the words we spoke. All words are recorded in heaven; yes, even the idle ones.

Jesus showed the power of the spoken faith.

> And Jesus answering saith unto them, Have faith in God. For verily I say unto you, That whosoever shall *say* unto this mountain, Be thou removed, and be thou cast into the sea; and shall *not doubt* in his heart, but shall believe that those things which he *saith* shall come to pass; he shall have *whatsoever he saith* (Mark 11:22-23).

The little woman with the issue of blood spoke her healing before she was healed. "For she said within herself, If I may but touch his garment, I shall be whole" (Matthew 9:21). She talked to herself. Jesus said, "Thy faith hath made thee whole." In other words, "The things you have spoken and believed have come to pass."

Whatever is spoken shall come to pass, if faith is accompanied with the spoken word. The words can be words of doubt or they can be words of faith. Whatsoever he says shall come to pass.

Jesus told the story about the man who went to his friend at midnight to ask of bread. The friend would not get up, so the man just kept knocking until his friend got up and gave him bread. He got what he asked for. Jesus ended the story with these words: "And I say unto you, Ask, and it shall be given you; seek, and ye shall find; knock, and it shall be opened unto you. For everyone that *asketh* receiveth; and he that seeketh findeth; and he that knock-eth it shall be opened" (Luke 11:9-10). Faith was in the voice, purpose, and the knock; faith received, found, and opened the door. Faith always receives and opens doors that are sealed shut.

Jesus told the people that their words formed their destiny. "But I say unto you, That every idle word that men shall speak, they shall give account thereof in the day of judgment, For by *thy words* thou shalt be justified, and by *thy words* thou shalt be condemned" (Matthew 12:36-37).

You can talk yourself into a miracle, or you can talk yourself out of a miracle. You can live by speaking words of faith, or you can write your own death sentence. Words such as these are words of doom: "I don't know what we're going to do. Everything's a mess!" "The doctors say I only have six months to live, so I'm getting my house in order." "We have tried everything, and nothing works. Everything just looks hopeless." On and on the expressions of doubt, fear, and unbelief speak forth from the lips of men and women daily on the face of the earth. No wonder there is such a negative feeling in the government, politics, homes, and schools. Everyone is speaking man's wisdom, and their eyes are on the circumstances. Few men and women have their minds and thoughts centered on the name of the Lord.

Listen to the conversation around you when there is a long line at the counter, or when everything looks gloomy in the world situation. Everyone joins in and speaks the same thing. Hopelessness, despair, gripes, complaints, anger, and everything negative in general.

The power of the spoken word is phenomenal! Examine the story of the twelve spies. When Moses sent them to spy out Canaan, they came back with two conflicting reports. Ten of the spies told the people that they were not able to take the land because of the giants.

And Caleb stilled the people before Moses, and *said,* Let us go up at once, and possess it; for we are well able to overcome it. But the men that went up with him *said,* We be not able to go up against the people; for they are stronger than we. And they brought up *an evil report* of the land which they had searched unto the children of Israel, *saying,* The land through which we have gone to search it, is a land that eateth up the inhabitants thereof; and all the people that we saw in it are men of a great stature. And there *we saw* the giants, the sons of Anak, which come of the giants: and we were in *our own sight* as grasshoppers, and so we were in their sight (Numbers 13:30-33).

They saw themselves as small, and so they believed their enemy saw them the same way. Their conception of themselves was rooted in their subconscious mind. Their future was mapped out according to their thoughts and conceptions. They had not spoken to the enemy, they just assumed this to be. Their eyes were focused on themselves instead of the power of their God. God had already spoken to them and told them He would give them the land. It was as good as done, but they did not believe the spoken word of God. They believed instead the apparent impossibilities.

Why does the general public like the negative report, and why does it listen to the negative instead of the positive?

This is exactly what happened in the case of the children of Israel. One speech against another speech. The negative are always the majority. The report of the ten spies was based on men's wisdom, and it influenced the people to cry out against their leader, Moses. When Joshua and Caleb saw the effect of the speech of the ten spies upon the people, they tried one more time to convince them that the report was not right.

> And they spake unto all the company of the children of Israel, saying, The land, which we passed through to search it, is an exceeding good land. If the Lord delight in us, then he will bring us into this land, and give it us; a land which floweth with milk and honey. Only rebel not ye against the Lord, neither fear ye the people of the land, for they are bread for us; their defence is departed from them, and the Lord is with us: fear them not (Numbers 14:7-9).

Powerful speech? It was so powerful that the children of Israel picked up stones and wanted to stone them. They did not want to hear the report of faith. They wanted to believe the evil report of doubt. God appeared at that precise moment to Moses in a glory cloud and God was angry because they did not have faith in Him.

And the Lord spake unto Moses and unto Aaron, saying, How long shall I bear with this *evil* congregation, which murmur against me? I have heard the murmurings of the children of Israel, which they murmur against me. Say unto them, As truly as I live, saith the Lord, as ye have *spoken in mine ears, so will I do to you.* Your carcasses shall fall in this wilderness...(Numbers 14:26-29).

God had two opinions about the two speeches. He said about Caleb, "But my servant Caleb, because he had another spirit with him, and hath followed me fully, him will I bring into the land..." (Numbers 14:24). Death came to those who gave the report of doubt. "Even those men that did bring up the *evil report* upon the land, died by the plague before the Lord" (Numbers 14:37). There are still two factions in the church--those that speak words of faith and those that speak words of doubt. Which side are you on?

Be careful what you speak. Words are as powerful as steel. They hammer into the consciousness of men and of God and form the basis of all actions. Wars are started by mere words. In the momentous hour when Nazism was just coming into existence, Hitler spoke to a group of people in a beer cellar in Munich. His inflammatory words, which bristled with hate, were mirrored in the hardened faces of the evil group, and soon they engulfed the world in war. An artist has portrayed the scene, putting on canvas the facial reactions of the group to Hitler's fiery words. He titled the painting, *In the Beginning Was the Word.*

People are estranged by words. Murders are committed because of violent words. The spoken word is as good as done, so be careful what you say.

Five words caused Zacharias to endure forty weeks of silence. When the angel appeared to him as he was executing the priest's office, he told him, "...Fear not, Zacharias: for thy prayer is heard; and thy wife Elizabeth shall bear thee a son, and thou shalt call his name John. And thou shalt have joy and gladness; and many shall rejoice at his birth. For he shall be great in the sight of the Lord..." (Luke 1:13-15).

The next moment in history was an important one. The next words spoken were words of destiny for Zacharias. His words would either be words of faith or words of doubt. What were they? "And Zacharias *said* unto the angel, *Whereby shall I know this?* for I am an old man, and my wife well stricken in years" (Luke 1:18). He just could not believe that this could be. It sounded too far-out or impossible.

Because of his words of unbelief, the angel told him, "...thou shalt be dumb, and not able to speak, until the day that these things shall be performed, because thou believest not my words..." (Luke 1:20). The people could not figure out what had happened to the priest. They wondered why he was taking so long, and when he came out he beckoned to them. They thought he had seen a vision because he was speechless. God took away the very thing that had caused his predicament in the first place: the power of the tongue to speak.

The power is in the tongue. "But what saith it? The *word* is nigh thee, even in thy *mouth,* and in thy heart: that is, the *word of faith,* which we preach" (Romans 10:8). You have to work at being able to speak words of faith, because man is naturally negative. The mind must be filled with the powerful Word of God, so that the extension of the mind, the tongue, can speak words of faith.

The Lord hears every single word that we speak. We either delight God's heart or we weary Him with our words. "Ye have wearied the Lord with your words" (Malachi 2:17). How refreshing it is for the Lord to hear a group gathered together for a prayer meeting speaking about what God is able to do and what God is going to do. His eyes are upon them whether they be in America, Korea, Africa, Europe, Asia, or any other part of the world. He smiles upon those of pure faith and gives them special visitations of the spirit. They are walking in a dimension of faith where to them everything is possible. They just believe that with God all things are possible, and the worse the situation, the greater the miracle will be. They do not talk about Aunt Mary's death when someone asks prayer for cancer. They pray in faith telling the cancer to be canceled in the name of the Lord Jesus and by the power of the blood. They do not equate circumstances with negative things in the past; they only apply the word and faith in the Word and believe for a miracle. These are the people that have the approval of God. He says about them as He said about Caleb, "They have another spirit."

The spirit of Joshua and Caleb was revealed by their words. Words are simply the mind speaking its contents.

The Lord wants his people to give blessing and not cursing. The mouth speaks these forth.

Finally, be ye all of one mind, having compassion one of another, love as brethren...not rendering evil for evil..but contrariwise blessing; knowing that ye are thereunto called that ye should inherit a blessing. For he that will love life, and see good days, let him refrain his tongue from evil...For the eyes of the Lord are over the righteous, and his ears are open unto their prayers; but the face of the Lord is against them that do evil (I Peter 3:8-12).

The children of Israel spoke their own curse. They could have chosen blessing, but their mouth brought the curse upon them. They did not bless one another, they cursed one another. Because of the evil speaking, they had to walk in the wilderness forty years. That was not the original plan of God, but they spoke it into existence. How many Christians today wander in the maze of a spiritual wilderness, and wonder why God never does things for them, and does everything for someone else? We need to all examine what we are filling our mind with, and what we are speaking. Anything that exalts itself against the knowledge of God is evil. Any thought or imagination that supersedes the Word of God must be brought down forcibly and replaced by power thoughts. Words of faith can be spoken from way down deep, but before that happens the fountain has got to be cleansed.

> Therewith bless we God, even the Father; and therewith curse we men, which are made after the similitude of God. Out of the same mouth proceedeth blessing and cursing. My brethren these things ought not to be. Doth a fountain send forth at the same place sweet water and bitter? (James 3:9-11).

Words only erupt out of the source. They are already in the mind before they are spoken. Liquid thoughts become words of substance. It is essential that the mind first be cleansed from fear and doubt in order to bless a world with the language of faith.

We must bless one another with words of faith. Before we speak words of faith, we must first believe. "We having the same spirit of faith, according as it is written, I believed, and therefore have I spoken; we also believe, and therefore speak" (II Corinthians 4:13).

Two weeks ago, I was heading home from church when I felt prompted by the spirit to go to a certain grocery store. The original plans were for me to go the following day, but such a strong feeling came over me to go that night that I turned the car around and went there immediately. The minute I got out of the car and started walking towards the store, I thought I saw someone familiar. I glanced away, but saw a lady who had just prayed through recently come walking hurriedly towards me. As soon as we got within speaking distance, she said, "Oh, Sister Haney, you are an angel. I just prayed that the Lord would send someone to encourage me. I just got word that my husband is leaving me for another woman and I am just devastated."

The presence of the Lord enveloped the two of us as I told her, "Honey, let's pray right now." We joined hands there in the parking lot and prayed a prayer of faith. We took authority and prayed against the evil work of Satan, the destroyer of marriages. Then I quoted to her Philippians 1:6 and Mark 11:22-24. She left with tears in her eyes but with faith in her heart, and said, "I feel so encouraged. I know God is going to answer our prayer."

As I drove away my whole body tingled with the presence of the Lord. He had sent me on a mission, and I had not let Him down. It was the greatest feeling in the world. No, I did not speak to a great audience, no bells were rung, but God was smiling on me. I felt it so strongly. It was the most glorious experience. This is what life is all about--speaking words of faith to all we meet, and pointing them to hope in Jesus Christ!

Chapter 13
Faith And Love

Faith operates in the highest dimension, which is love. In the incident of the fig tree, when Jesus was telling the people they could have whatever they desired if they would only believe and not doubt, He did not stop there. The very next phrase says, "And when ye stand praying, forgive, if ye have ought against any: that your Father also which is in heaven may forgive you your trespasses. But if ye do not forgive, neither will your Father which is in heaven forgive your trespasses" (Mark 11:25-26).

Jesus said that when you are praying for your miracle all feelings of resentment, grudges, ill-will, jealousy, and dislike against *any* must be taken out of the heart and forgiveness must take their place. Faith is blocked by anger, bitterness, or hate. Many times in the scriptures, faith and charity, or faith and love, have been coupled together. They are inseparable.

Here are just a few of them:

Wherefore I also, after I heard of your *faith* in the Lord Jesus, and *love* unto all the saints (Ephesians 1:15).

Since we heard of your *faith* in Christ Jesus, and of the *love* which ye have to all the saints (Colossians 1:4).

Remembering without ceasing your work of *faith,* and labour of *love*... (I Thessalonians 1:3).

...Timotheus came from you unto us, and brought us good tidings of your *faith* and *charity*... (I Thessalonians 3:6).

It is interesting to note the historical setting of the time Paul wrote to the church at Thessalonica, around A.D. 55.

Notice he writes, "We are bound to thank God always for you, brethren, as it is meet, because that your *faith* groweth exceedingly, and the *charity* of every one of you all toward each other aboundeth" (II Thessalonians 1:3). He goes on to say that he knows they are going through persecutions, but he glories in their patience and faith. Notice as charity abounded, faith grew exceedingly!

Edward Gibbon published a book in 1776 entitled, *The Decline and Fall of the Roman Empire.* It is said that this is the most correct and majestic work of history ever written, and bridges the abyss between the ancient and modern worlds. According to Gibbon, the church was going through heavy persecutions, but at the same time they were having great miracles. What was the atmosphere between the saints at this time? Gibbon says,

> Doubtless there were many among the primitive Christians of a temper more suitable to the meekness and charity of their profession. There were many who felt a sincere compassion for the danger of their friends and countrymen, and who exerted the most benevolent zeal to save them from the impending destruction.

Some of Paul's writings were written during the reign of Nero. It was during this time that Christians suffered outrageously under his hand. "Some were nailed on crosses; others sewn up in the skins of wild beasts, and exposed to the fury of dogs; others again, smeared over with combustible materials, were used as torches to illuminate the darkness of the night." As the persecutions escalated, so did the faith and love of the Christians.

It has already been mentioned in Chapter 3 of the power of the early church and the miracles that were taking place. Not only were they suffering persecutions, but they were praying, fasting, and having great miracles while love was growing among them. Suffering combined with prayer and fasting always cleans out the "junk." When your head is being cut off, you don't care about petty things. When a Christian is burning at the stake, his mind is on where he is going, not on who did this or who did that. As love increases, then faith can operate.

When people get together and start praying, something happens. They can enter the meeting place with bad feelings toward one another, but after praying together and letting the love of God flow through them, walls are broken down and miracles begin to occur. Love, tears, humility, and forgiveness always touch God and get His attention. As people humble themselves and pray, God is then exalted among them, for He dwells only with the humble. Where God is, there are miracles.

Paul writes, "But let us, who are of the day, be sober, putting on the breastplate of *faith and love...*" (I Thessalonians 5:8). Faith and love will protect the heart from the wounds of the enemy. They will keep you healthy spiritually, and enable you to fight more effectively. Right before Paul's martyrdom, at the height of the persecution, he writes to Philemon and mentions again the atmosphere that was among the church.

> Hearing of thy love and faith, which thou hast toward the Lord Jesus, and toward all saints; That the communication of thy faith may become effectual by the acknowledging of every good thing which is in you in Christ Jesus, For we have great joy and consolation in thy love, because the bowels of the saints are refreshed by thee, brother (Philemon 1:5-7).

Faith alone in itself will come to nought. Faith must be accompanied by love, for Paul said, "And now abideth faith, hope, charity, these three; but the greatest of these is charity" (I Corinthians 13:13). I have thought often on this passage, and have come to the conclusion that love is the greatest, but without faith in God one cannot have true love. It is written, "But without faith it is impossible to please him; for he that cometh to God must believe that he is, and that he is a rewarder of them that diligently seek him" (Hebrews 11:6). God is love, and in order to know God and His love, there first must be faith. Faith and love are inseparable. They belong together. There is a certain faith generated by man that can be used for self-glory and a misuse of power, and the wrong kind of love can destroy. Hitler had an inner conviction that he could conquer nations, but he destroyed people with his belief. He had self-love, but hated the Jews. His twisted faith and love abused and trampled, but when faith and love are connected with true love, which is God, great and wondrous things transpire. Faith has to be in existence for love to be able to be released into proper channels. There has to be the connection between them. This kind of faith and love always edifies and lifts people up to a higher plane. The faith and love that is given from above is different than what man generates from within his own mind.

God is concerned about people loving people and speaking words of faith to one another. He wants His people to be healthy spiritually and physically, and to live in victory.

There are four major "above alls" in the New Testament. They have to do with love, faith, and health. They are:

Beloved, I wish *above all* things, that thou mayest prosper and be in health, even as thy soul prospereth (III John 2).

And *above all* things have fervent charity among yourselves: for charity shall cover the multitude of sins (I Peter 4:8).

And *above all* these things, put on charity, which is the bond of perfectness (Colossians 3:14).

The fourth "above all" brings us to the next chapter.

Chapter 14
Shield of Faith

Ephesians 6:16 says, *"Above all,* taking the shield of faith, wherewith ye shall be able to quench all the fiery darts of the wicked." Christians many times flip this verse off their tongue like an old familiar saying, but when it comes to putting it into practice, they are not aware of how to do it.

First of all, what is a shield? It is a broad piece of defensive armor, consisting of a frame of metal, and carried on the arm or held in the hand by a handle. It is a protection against something. It is used to ward off, to defend, or to cover from danger. It is important to the offense, because when the warrior moves forward, the shield protects him from the enemy. The New Testament, which was written in Greek, refers to Grecian armor. The Greeks used both round and oval shields which were heavy and almost covered the body. The shield in modern warfare is the armor-plate covering installed around a gun to protect the gun's crew from enemy fire.

Christians are protected by God's impartation of faith to them. The thing to remember is that the devil does not have the power to obliterate; he only has his painful irritating darts. He cannot win against you unless you let him. The devil may have his darts, but Christians have a sword. Those darts might have fire in them, and one might get by the shield, and it will burn, hurt, inflame, and cause one to scream with pain, but "Beloved, think it not strange concerning the fiery trial which is to try you, as though some strange thing happened unto you: But rejoice, inasmuch as ye are partakers of Christ's sufferings; that when his glory shall be revealed, ye may be glad also with exceeding joy" (I Peter 4:12-13).

Rejoice, because if you were not linked up with God, the devil would not be bothering you so much, and not only for that reason, but rejoice because you are going to win. It may look like the devil is winning, but with God there is always another move.

In the early part of the last century an artist, who was also a great chess player, painted a picture of a chess game. The players consisted of a young man and Satan. The young man was playing the white pieces, while the devil had the black. The reason for the game was that if the young man won he would be free of the power of evil, but if the devil won the man was to be his slave forever.

The artist believed in the supreme power of evil and presented the devil as victor. In the picture the young man's hand hovered over his rook, his face paled with amazement--there was no hope. The devil won. For years the picture hung in an art gallery. Finally one day a chess player started to doubt the picture. He studied the picture and became convinced that there was but one chess player upon the earth who could give him assurance that the artist of this picture was not right in his conception of the winner. The chess player was the aged Paul Morphy, a resident of New Orleans, Louisiana. Morphy was a supreme master of chess in his day, an undefeated champion.

Morphy stood before the picture five minutes, ten minutes, twenty minutes, thirty minutes. He was all concentration; he lifted and lowered his hands, as in imagination, he made and eliminated moves. Suddenly, his hand paused, his eyes burned with the vision of an unthought-of combination. Suddenly, he shouted, "Young man, make that move. That's the move."

To the amazement of all, the old master, the chess authority, had discovered a combination that the creating artist had not considered. The young man defeated the devil after all. The end result is what counts in chess as well as with the battle over the evil one. Winning is what it is all about. There has to be a battle or a challenge before there can be a victory. Shields are not needed at tea parties, only on battlefields.

When you sign up to be in the army of the Lord, you enlist into the battle of all time. The General hands out the equipment and the shield is one of the major pieces of equipment, for without it you are dead, but with it you win. Faith in God never loses. It is guaranteed victory.

Faith is tried and developed through hardship, disappointment, disillusionment, conflict, frustration, and failure. If you never had a problem, how could you see

God's miraculous power at work? Faith is developed through exercise. Faith is not gained by looking at beautiful stained glass windows and padded pews. When your back is up against the wall, you need something more than nice-sounding phrases. Faith is the vision of the heart. It sees God in the dark, as in the day.

Abraham, already mentioned in this book, was a man of faith. What was it that set him apart from other men? First of all, when God spoke to him in Genesis 12, Abraham obeyed Him without question, and then built an altar. The second time God appeared to him in chapter 13, and told him that his seed would be as the dust of the earth, he built another altar. The third time God appeared to him, he said to Abraham these powerful words: "...Fear not, Abram; I am thy *shield,* and thy exceeding great reward" (Genesis 15:1).

Notice after the Lord had told him his seed would also be as the stars of the heaven and the sands of the sea, verse 6 says, "And he believed in the Lord...." When faith is present in God, and man believes everything God says, then God draws near to man and connects with his faith and becomes a shield of faith to the believer. Faith is not hard when God is a part of it.

The reason God could trust Abraham was because he always obeyed, no matter what. God appeared to Abraham again in chapter 17. That is when he laughed in his heart, because he was 99 years old. Then the Lord appeared to him in chapter 18, and after communing with the angels as well, he and the Lord communed about the destruction of Sodom. But before He talked with Abraham about the city, He made a statement to the two angels that gave a clue as to why God trusted Abraham so much. The Lord said, "For *I know him,* that he will command his children, and his household after him, and they shall keep the way of the Lord, to do justice and judgment..." (Genesis 18:19). The Lord knew him and had confidence in him that he would obey Him fully with his whole heart.

The Lord had one more test for Abraham to see if he would obey blindly as he had done before. His first test was to see if he would give up family, home, lands, prestige, riches--just everything! Then God asked him to give up his son on an altar of sacrifice. He passed the second test, for when Isaac was on the altar, Abraham drew back the knife to plunge it into the heart of his only son. The angel of the Lord called and said, "Lay not thine hand upon the lad, neither do thou any thing unto him: *for now I know,* that thou fearest God, seeing thou hast not withheld thy son, thine only son from me" (Genesis 22:12).

The clue to the close relationship between God and Abraham and all the blessings was obedience. "And in thy seed shall all thy nations of the earth be blessed; *because thou hast obeyed my voice"* (Genesis 22:18). Abraham had such a close relationship with God, as well as several encounters with angels, that it was a natural way to live. It was his lifestyle. So when he called his eldest servant to go get a wife for Isaac, he thought nothing about taking authority and telling him that the angel of the Lord would go before him when the servant questioned about whether the woman would return with him. Abraham said, "The Lord God of heaven, which took me from my father's house, and from the land of my kindred, and which spake unto me, and that sware unto me saying, Unto thy seed will I give this land;" (Note: Abraham was so used to believing that he did not doubt this either.) "This same God that spoke these things will send his angel before thee..." (Genesis 24:7).

The shield of faith held in the believer's hand cannot be seen. When you get dressed in the morning and put your shoes on, you can see, touch, and smell them. But you cannot see, touch, or smell faith. You think, "If I could just see this shield, pick it up and put it down, and know that it is there--how much easier it would be." No, then it would be harder; you would be limiting yourself, because the spirit world is so much greater than the touchable world. Faith is very invisible, but very tangible. It believes without question, performs without hesitation, and is supported by all of heaven. The shield of faith is not decorative, but is used in pushing back hell, doubt, and disease.

Somehow Christians must have their eyes opened to the fact of how powerful God and His resources are. He has all power. He Himself is enough, but He gives even more than Himself. He gives to His children the Word, Spirit, the power of His Blood, His Name, His abiding Presence, and the help of His angelic host. These angels are present in the heavens, and by the side of the believer, or wherever God sends them.

If you have difficulty believing that angels are ready to help you, then you will have difficulty believing in God, for He uses them constantly to do His bidding. Only the sad you see, do not believe in the angels. "For the Sadducees say that there is no resurrection, neither angel, nor spirit..." (Acts 23:8).

Angels are referred to often in the scripture, and one of their purposes is given in Hebrews.

> But to which of the angels said he at any time, Sit on my right hand, until I make thine enemies thy footstool? Are they not all *ministering spirits,* sent forth to minister for them who shall be heirs of salvation? But ye are come unto mount Sion, and unto the city of the living God, the heavenly Jerusalem, and to an *innumerable company of angels* (Hebrews 1:14; 12:22).

The whole thing boils down to this: Why should we be afraid to step out by faith, when we have so much power on our side?

When Peter was put in prison, the people did not despair, they prayed. "Peter therefore was kept in prison: but prayer was made without ceasing of the church unto God for him" (Acts 12:5). The church had the shield of faith and they were pushing back hell with it. While the church warred in the spirit, Peter slept.

"And behold, the angel of the Lord came upon him, and a light shined in the prison: and he smote Peter on the side, and raised him up, saying, Arise up quickly. And his chains fell off from his hands" (Acts 12:7). Peter did not even realize it was an angel. He thought it was a vision. Sometimes we have heavenly visitations, and we are like Peter--unaware. He finally recognized it for what it was. "And when Peter was *come to himself,* he said, Now I know of a surety, that the Lord hath sent his angel, and hath delivered me out of the hand of Herod..." (Acts 12:11).

The prayer and faith of the church connected with the power of God became Peter's shield. He protected him from the enemy's scheme. The shield is not just a piece of metal you hold in your hand. No! It cannot be separated from God. It is God's weaponry He gives you. He expects us to lean upon Him and fuse our faith with His power and have signs, wonders, and miracles.

Chapter 15

When Belief (or Man's Faith) is Not Enough

The evil spiritual kingdom can only be ruled and dominated by God's spirit; man's spirit is not enough. Man and woman are spirits; their bodies are only shells of what they are. The human body will return to dust, but the spirit will live on. It is a powerful spirit that dwells in man, but it is not powerful enough to subdue demonic spirits. This is proven several times in the scripture. One particular place is found in the book of Acts.

Then certain of the vagabond Jews, exorcists, took upon them to call over them which had evil spirits the name of the Lord Jesus, saying, We adjure you by Jesus whom Paul preacheth, And the evil spirit answered and said, Jesus I know, and Paul I know; but who are ye? And the man in whom the evil spirit was leaped on them, and overcame them, and prevailed against them, so that they fled out of that house naked and wounded (Acts 19:13-16).

They believed they could do it, but belief was not enough. Another incident of failure over demons took place with the disciples of Christ. They tried to cast a demon out of a son that fell into the fire and had no control over himself at times. The father uttered these words in Luke 9:40: "And I besought thy disciples to cast him out; and they could not."

They believed they could do it, or they would have never tried to cast the demon out, but they were unable to do it. As much as they believed, the kind of faith they had was not enough.

So what is the answer? How can one have the kind of faith to be able to subdue evil spirits and cast demons out? Jesus gave the answer Himself, although some modernists try to prove Jesus wrong. He said it in simple terms. It sounds simple, but it is discipline to the flesh. Many people want the miracles of the early church, but are unwilling to pay the price.

The words of Jesus are so plain, even a child could understand them. Why do people try to put another meaning on them? "Jesus said unto him, If thou canst believe, all things are possible to him that believeth" (Mark 9:23).

Jesus spoke those words after the father of the child had gone to the disciples for help, and they could not help. He then brought his son to Jesus. "...Straightway the spirit tare him; and he fell on the ground, and wallowed foaming. And he asked his father, How long is it ago since this came unto him? And he said, Of a child. And ofttimes it hath cast him into the fire, and into the waters, to destroy him:

but if thou canst do anything, have compassion on us, and help us" (Mark 9:20-22).

After Jesus rebuked the foul deaf and dumb spirit to come out of him, the disciples asked Him privately, "Why could not we cast him out?" Jesus never spoke idle words. When He spoke they were words of eternal life and potent words of instruction. Listen carefully to what Jesus said:

And he said unto them, This kind can come forth by nothing, but by prayer and fasting (Mark 9:29).

Some modernists are teaching heresy when they say the church does not need to pray and fast in this generation. This is not scriptural; it is diabolical. Beware of those who encourage you not to pray. They will cause you to lose power and maybe your soul. Prayer is as essential to the Christian as breathing is to the natural man. If you do not develop a prayer life, you will be weak, shallow, and powerless. You may preach high-sounding words, but your words will be cold. There will not be the hot breath of the anointing that makes people weep and be influenced towards Christ. Cold logic will not stand before the judgment seat of Christ. What will stand is the Word of God that has not been explained away or watered down by intelligent analytical minds.

The reason why there are so many weak Christians is because they are trying to do it in their own power and their own mind faith. That is not enough. Man cannot generate enough faith by just reading the Word. "...for the letter killeth, but the spirit giveth life" (I Corinthians 3:6).

The Word of God is powerful and it does give faith, but faith comes by more than the Word. Faith comes by three things, and as it is exercised, it increases.

1. The Word of God. "So then faith cometh by hearing, and hearing by the word of God" (Romans 10:17).

2. Prayer. "But ye, beloved, building up yourselves on your most holy faith, praying in the Holy Ghost" (Jude 1:20).

3. Fasting. See Mark 9:29 above.

The contact with the Spirit of God imparts faith unto man. People contact God through the three things above. It all starts with humbling yourself from your intellect to the acknowledgment of the intellect of God. How does one humble himself? God told the people in the Old Testament if they would humble themselves and pray He would heal their land. David made the statement, "I humbled my soul with fasting" (Psalm 35:13). Prayer and fasting bring you into a realm of the spirit and the Word of God gives you the direction and truth to know what to do with the power of the spirit. The three are inseparable. (Note: If you are interested in further study on fasting and prayer, order the books *When Ye Fast* and *When Ye Pray* by this author, Joy Haney.)

Do you want to know firsthand what the early church was doing shortly after the ascension of Christ? Some of these were the original followers of Christ and had heard Him speak to them in person. Following is an excerpt from Gibbon's *The Decline and Fall of the Roman Empire:*

The Christian church, from the time of the apostles and their disciples, has claimed an uninterrupted succession of miraculous powers, the gift of tongues, of vision, and of prophecy, the power of expelling demons, of healing the sick, and of raising the dead. The divine inspiration, whether it was conveyed in the form of a waking or a sleeping vision, is described as a favor very liberally bestowed on all ranks of the faithful, on women as on elders, on boys as well as upon bishops. When their devout minds were sufficiently prepared by a course of prayer, of fasting, and of vigils, to receive the extraordinary impulse, they were transported out of their senses, and delivered in *extasy* what was inspired, being mere organs of the Holy Spirit, just as a pipe or flute is of him who blows into it. The expulsion of the demons from the bodies of those unhappy persons whom they had been permitted to torment was considered as a signal though ordinary triumph of religion, and is repeatedly alleged by the ancient apologists as the most convincing evidence of the truth of Christianity. But the miraculous cure of diseases of the most inveterate or even preternatural kind can no longer occasion any surprise, when we recollect that in the days of Irenaeus, about the end of the second century, the resurrection of the dead was very far from being esteemed an uncommon event; that the miracle was frequently performed on necessary occasions, by great fasting and the joint supplication of the church of the place, and that the persons thus restored to their prayers had lived afterwards amongst them many years. The primitive Christians perpetually trod on mystic ground, and their minds were exercised by, the habits of believing the most extraordinary events. They felt, or they fancied, that on every side they were incessantly assaulted by demons, comforted by visions, instructed by prophecy, and surprisingly delivered from danger, sickness, and from death itself, by the supplications of the church.

This was the primitive church, the Christians that lived following the ascension of Christ. Does this sound like the twentieth-century church? We need to repent, go back to the humble way, and adopt a lifestyle that Jesus intended us to live if we want to have the miracles of the early church.

Some would have the church do away with prayer and fasting because there is confusion on the part of some as to exactly what Paul was talking about in Galatians 2:21: "I do not frustrate the grace of God: for if righteousness come by the law, then Christ is dead in vain." They feel as if Paul is doing away with things that man would do himself. This is entirely wrong.

The big misunderstanding of the early church concerned circumcision. Go back to verse three and you will see that this is what Paul is addressing. Verse four says that false brethren came to spy on our liberty, that they might bring us into bondage. Verse seven explains what the controversy was about: the gospel of circumcision and the gospel of uncircumcision. He is still talking about circumcision in Galatians 5:11 and in Galatians 6:2. Galatians was written in A.D. 60 during Paul's third visit to Corinth. This was during the time that Gibbon described. The law does not deal with prayer and fasting. There was no argument whatsoever about the subject of prayer and fasting. It was the accepted way. Everyone did it, including Jesus Christ Himself, the great example. Circumcision had been a matter of salvation and was required by God in the Old Testament, but the New Testament church was not required to be circumcised. This was the point of controversy. It was hard for the Jews to give up the doctrine of circumcision. Nowhere does the scripture say that prayer and fasting were done away with. Love was the new law, not legalism. Love is the constraining force that will cause men and women to give themselves to the things of the spirit.

Galatians 2:1 says that Paul and Barnabas went to Jerusalem. Look also in Acts 13:2,3 and see what they were doing. They were praying and fasting. The Book of Acts was written around the same time Galatians was written. Paul would not have practiced one thing and have been so foolish as to speak against it to the Galatians. Notice also in II Corinthians 11:27 that Paul names the things he went through for the gospel's sake. He lists forced hunger separately from fasting. There is a difference. Fasting is voluntary.

Paul would have never told the husbands and wives to take time to give themselves to prayer and fasting in I Corinthians 7, and then turn around and contradict himself in Galatians. No! God forbid that modern-day preachers would have the gall to explain the words of Jesus away and put words in Paul's mouth. He himself made many statements as to his own discipline of the flesh. The flesh will dominate if man allows it to do so. You do not fight flesh with flesh. You fight the works of the flesh with the spirit. Listen to him as he talks about the war between flesh and spirit, and how he conquered:

> For they that are after the flesh, do mind the things of the flesh; but they that are after the Spirit the things of the Spirit. For to be carnally minded is death; but to be spiritually minded is life and peace...For if ye live after the flesh, ye shall die; but if ye through the Spirit do mortify the deeds of the body, ye shall live (Romans 8:5-6, 12-13).

Paul summarizes the responsibility of the ministry in II Corinthians 6: "But in all things approving ourselves as the ministers of God, in much patience...in fastings." He also said he was "...in fastings often" (II Corinthians 11:27). Remember, Paul was one the Christians referred to in the historical account of Gibbon. Paul said, "I am crucified with Christ: nevertheless I live; yet not I, but Christ liveth in me: and the life which I now live in the flesh I live by the faith of the Son of God, who loved me, and gave himself for me" (Galatians 2:20).

When someone asked Jesus what it took to be a disciple of His, He gave them this key:

...If any man will come after me, let him deny himself, and take up his cross daily, and follow me. For whosoever will save his life, shall lose it; but whosoever will lose his life for my sake, the same shall save it (Luke 9:23-24).

If anyone would say that daily prayer and times of fasting are not necessary then they are either deceived or ignorant. They elevate themselves above Jesus and Paul and make a mockery of the early church. Only the foolish would argue and do away with the blatant historical and biblical evidence of the practice of the early church which was following the teachings of Christ.

If the church wants the same kind of miracles happening in this day, then it will have to do the same things the early church did. Belief is not enough to raise the dead, cast out demons, and do other miraculous things. Man must go beyond what he thinks can happen, but he must make it happen. He cannot do it while living in the realm of natural or carnal thinking. The only way to ascend into the realm of the miraculous is to become saturated with the thoughts and spirit of Christ.

One cannot spend all day reading a fiction novel and become empowered with the spirit from on high. The only way to become endued with power from on high is to sit in prayer in the presence of the Lord. If the flesh beckons louder than the spirit, then it is time to fast away the desires of the flesh. Just as man can fast his way to physical health, he also can fast himself to spiritual health. The five senses become deadened so that the spirit can dominate.

The spirit within becomes disassociated from the demands of the body; therefore, it can focus on God and the Word, bringing it into a higher dimension of the Spirit.

A quote from Athenaeus, the Greek physician, bears this out: "Fasting cures diseases, dries up bodily tumors, puts demons to flight, gets rid of impure thoughts, makes the mind clearer and the heart purer, the body sanctified, and raises man to the throne of God."

Tertullian, the well-respected Roman theologian made this statement: "If practiced with the right intention, it makes man a friend of God. The demons are aware of that." You are either mocked by the underworld or feared by it as your relationship decreases or increases with God. If you want the power that the disciples lacked in Mark 9--the power that Paul had--you must do as Jesus said. Pray, fast and continue in His Word; then, and only then, will the church have the faith that they so desire to have.

Chapter 16
Faith to be Healed

The church is given direction what to do when there is sickness.

> Is any sick among you? let him call for the elders of the church; and let them pray over him, anointing him with oil in the *name* of the Lord: And the *prayer of faith* shall save the sick, and the *Lord* shall raise him up; and if he have committed sins, they shall be forgiven him (James 5:14-15).

Then also every believer is given power to "lay hands on the sick and they shall recover" (Mark 16:18).

If they shall recover, then why do some die? Let us examine this carefully. Please, stay with me until the end of the chapter.

First of all, I looked in the four gospels and there is not one place where Jesus ever turned anyone away without being healed when they asked Him to heal them. This was one of the reasons for His suffering. He purchased salvation for lost humanity by His death on the cross and the stripes on His back were for healing. Several places it mentions He healed them all.

And Jesus went about all Galilee, teaching in their synagogues, and preaching the gospel of the kingdom, and healing all manner of sickness and all manner of disease among the people. And his fame went throughout all Syria: and they brought unto him all sick people that were taken with divers diseases and torments, and those which were lunatic, and those that had the palsy; and *he healed them* (Matthew 4:23-24).

And Jesus went about all the cities and villages, teaching in their synagogues, and preaching the gospel of the kingdom, and healing *every* sickness and *every* disease among the people (Matthew 9:35).

But when Jesus knew it, he withdrew himself from thence: and great multitudes followed him, and he *healed them all* (Matthew 12:15).

Now when the sun was setting, all they that had any sick with divers diseases brought them unto him; and he laid his hands on *every* one of them, and healed them (Luke 4:40).

Everyone that asked, received. Over and over Jesus said, "According to your faith be it unto you." They believed, and were healed.

Secondly, I heard someone quote Hebrews 11:32-40, particularly verse 37, "They were...afflicted," and then say, "Yes, some of them died in their sicknesses even when they had faith." I wondered about this, so I looked up every scripture in the whole Bible that had to do with *affliction, afflictions,* and *afflicted.* Sure enough, it was not the way it had been presented to me. I found out that *affliction* in the scripture referred to mental distress, adversity, calamity, trouble, misfortune or hardship, which brought on a state of pain and grief of mind. The only place it could have been remotely tied in with sickness was in the case of Job. "So went Satan forth from the presence of the Lord, and smote Job with sore boils from the sole of his foot unto his crown" (Job 2:7). After reading the scriptures associated with Job and his affliction, it appears that the sickness brought him the distress and anguish of mind. (See details about Job later.) Some of the instances that show people who were afflicted are as follows:

Hagar in Genesis 16:11: "...The Lord hath heard thine affliction..." (Mental distress)

Leah in Genesis 29:32: "The Lord hath looked upon my affliction; now therefore my husband will love me..." (Mental anguish)

Jacob in Genesis 31:42: "...God hath seen mine afflictions..." (Mental distress)

Joseph in Genesis 41:52: "...For God hath made me to be fruitful in the land of my affliction." (Great mental distress and anguish)

Notice: ALL OF THE ABOVE FELT REJECTION.

The Children of Israel in Exodus 3:7: "...I will bring you up out of the affliction of Egypt..." (Heavy oppression)

Hannah in I Samuel 1:11: "...if thou wilt indeed look on the affliction of thine handmaiden..." (Distress caused by a childless womb)

Jerusalem in Lamentations 1:7: "Jerusalem remembered in the days of her affliction and of her miseries all her pleasant things that she had in the days of old, when her people fell into the hands of the enemy, and none did help her..." (The mind remembered and connected the enemy with her misery and affliction)

The Children of Israel in Exodus 1:12: "But the more they afflicted them, the more they multiplied and grew." (Their physical strength was not diminished, but their mental anguish was increased.)

Moses in Numbers 11:11: "...wherefore hast thou afflicted thy servant...that thou layest the *burden* of all this people upon me?" (The burden caused him mental distress)

Naomi in Ruth 1:21: "I went out full, and the Lord hath brought me home again empty...And the Almighty hath afflicted me." (This was a physically strong woman who had just walked many miles--her mind was in anguish and distress)

Jesus in Isaiah 53:7: "He was oppressed, and he was afflicted, yet he opened not his mouth..." (Jesus never was physically sick)

Paul in Colossians 1:24: "Who now rejoice in my suffering for you, and fill up that which is behind of the afflictions of Christ in my flesh for his body's sake, which is the church." (The Greek word for *afflictions* here is *thlipsis,* meaning "tribulation, distress, afflicted with trouble.")

Paul in II Corinthians 2:4: "For out of much affliction and anguish of heart I write unto you with many tears..." (Affliction is always associated with tears, hurt, trouble, confusion, oppression, anguish)

Jonah in Jonah 2:2: "...I cried by reason of mine affliction unto the Lord,...out of the belly of hell cried I..."

Job in Job 10:15: "...I am full of confusion; therefore, see my afflictions." (Confusion about why all this was happening brought distress of mind)

James makes a distinction. "Is any among you afflicted? let him pray. Is any merry? let him sing psalms. Is any sick..." (James 5:13).

So from this study it is concluded that the word *afflicted* in Hebrews 11:37 did not mean sickness. How could God contradict Himself? If He said the prayer of faith would raise up the sick, how could He let the people that had faith die? Before you respond, let us continue.

The Bible says that Jesus has the keys to hell and death (Revelation 1:18). Jesus has the final say on who dies and who lives. It is in His hands, but many times we have something to say about it also. It is a fact, confirmed by doctors, that 80% of all sickness is stress-related, and also that fear will kill a patient sometimes quicker than the disease itself. (Stress and fear are both products of the mind.) Death is promised to all, but sometimes there is premature death. This is not written to condemn, or determine the destiny of anyone; it is only written to give hope to those that encounter sickness and disease. Sickness and disease will come to many. What do you do with them when they come? Go to the Word and find the answers and then leave the rest in His hands, for He doeth all things well.

SPIRITUAL STEPS TO HEALING

1. Have someone anoint you with oil and pray for you. (James 5:14-15; Mark 16:17-18)

2. Confess your faults; repent and humble yourself. Care for one another.

The verse immediately after James 5:15 is in conjunction with healing: "Confess your faults one to another, and pray for one another, that ye may be healed. The effectual fervent prayer of a righteous man availeth much" (James 5:16).

Notice this is what happened to Job. First, he was self-righteous. "So these three men ceased to answer Job, because he was righteous in his own eyes" (Job 32:1). Then after all of Job's questioning, the Lord answered Job. "Who is this that darkeneth counsel by words without knowledge? Gird up thy loins like a man; for I will demand of thee, and answer thou me. Where wast thou when I laid the foundations of the earth? declare, if thou hast understanding" (Job 38:2-4).

On and on went the Lord showing Job that his arrogant know-it-all reasoning and questioning was puny compared to God's understanding. When God got through, "Then Job answered the Lord, and said, Behold I am vile, what shall I answer thee? I will lay mine hand upon my mouth" (Job 40:3-4).

After Job repented and prayed for his friends, God turned everything around for him. Job said, "I have heard of thee by the hearing of the ear: but now mine eye seeth thee. Wherefore I abhor myself, and repent in dust and ashes...And the Lord turned the captivity of Job, when he *prayed for his friends:* also the Lord gave Job twice as much as he had before" (Job 42:5,6,10).

3. Forgive anyone who has offended you. Forgive past hurts, abuse, or wrongs.

When Jesus told them in Mark 11:14 that they could have anything they desired if they would just believe, the very next sentence said, "When ye stand praying, forgive."

Jesus knew that the body cannot be healed with resentments, anger, grudges, bitterness, envy, pride, hate, and other like feelings or thoughts. The mind is intertwined with the physical; they are not separate from one another--one effects the other.

When Paul was explaining to them about the order of communion, he told them that some were sickly and weak among them and even died because they did not discern the Lord's body (I Corinthians 11:29-30). The body is the church. "And he is the head of the body, the church" (Colossians 1:18).

It is impossible to be filled with negative feelings and be totally healthy. The book *None of These Diseases,* written by Dr. S.I. McMillen, states:

> Emotional stress can cause high blood pressure, toxic goiter, migraine headaches, arthritis, apoplexy, heart trouble, gastrointestinal ulcers, and other serious diseases too numerous to mention. As physicians we can prescribe medicine for the symptoms of these diseases, but we can not do much for the underlying cause--emotional turmoil. It is lamentable that peace does not come in capsules.
>
> When Jesus said, "Forgive seventy times seven," He was thinking not only of our souls, but of saving our bodies from ulcerative colitis, toxic goiters, high blood pressure, and scores of other diseases...The famous physiologist, John Hunter, knew what anger could do to his heart: "The first scoundrel that gets me angry will kill me." Some time later, at a medical meeting, a speaker made assertions that incensed Hunter. As he stood up and bitterly attacked the speaker, his anger caused such a contraction of the blood vessels in his heart that he fell dead.

Jesus gave the prescription in Matthew 5:43-44 that would make us healthy spiritually and physically. "Ye have heard that it hath been said, Thou shalt love thy neighbour, and hate thine enemy. But I say unto you, Love your enemies, bless them that curse you, do good to them that hate you, and pray for them which despitefully use you, and persecute you." Baking pies not only for the family, but for those that have said evil things against you, is the way to peace. Forgiveness is always the way up to blessing.

4. Have child-like faith in the Word and in God.
"...by whose stripes ye were healed" (I Peter 2:24). The work was done at Calvary. Believe that He is the Lord God that heals all sickness and disease.

5. Fast your way to health, as is shown in Isaiah 58. (See also the book, *When Ye Fast* by this author, Joy Haney.)

PHYSICAL STEPS TO HEALING

We struggle to do good. We live under the curse of the Garden of Eden, and sickness will always be on the earth until the end of time. God has given us the promise of healing, and He heals us in spite of our bad habits, heredity, and weaknesses, but He also expects us to be good stewards of our health and the things that He has given us.

1. Work with God.
    A. Adopt good health habits, morally and physical-ly. If one willfully abuses his body, the temple, he sins

against his own body and works against his own state of health. Paul states this in I Corinthians 6:18, "Flee fornication. Every sin that a man doeth is without the body; but he that committeth fornication sinneth against his own body." The body of man is to glorify Christ, and habits which defile the body or weaken it work against the purpose of heaven. Laws are not given to be broken or to inflict punishment; they are given so that man can be blessed. God's health and spiritual laws cannot be violated without there being a cause and effect. Every act reaps a reward, whether good or bad.

    B. Develop an understanding of proper nutrition and have discipline to stick with it.

    C. Realize the importance of exercise. (If you have two legs, you can help walk your way to health.) It does wonders for the emotional, as well as the physical.

    D. Find something that you enjoy doing and make time to do it once a week. Do not live constantly under strain.

    E. Get proper rest. You are the steward of your life. If you are running on nervous energy because of hectic time schedules, then you *must* stop, evaluate, and wait on the Lord for new direction. It is not the will of God to live rushed, worried, fretful lives.

    2. Speak positive things. Do away with gossip and negative talk.

    A. Proverbs 18:21: "Death and life are in the power of the tongue..."

B. Proverbs 12:18: "...the tongue of the wise is health."

C. Proverbs 16:24: "Pleasant words are as an honeycomb, sweet to the soul, and health to the bones."

D. Proverbs 15:30: "...a good report maketh the bones fat."

3. Think healthy thoughts

A. Proverbs 14:30: "The light of the eyes rejoiceth the heart." Whatever you read or see conveys information into your brain and effects your physical and spiritual heart.

B. Proverbs 3:8: "It shall be health to thy navel, and marrow to thy bones." What shall be? The getting of wisdom.

C. Proverbs 14:30: "A sound heart is the life of the flesh: but envy the rottenness of the bones." Negative feelings bring disease into the body.

D. Joshua 1:8: "Meditate on the law of the Lord day and night and ye shall have good success and be prosperous."

4. Laugh often. Proverbs 17:22: "A merry heart doeth good like a medicine; but a broken spirit drieth the bones."

5. Relax; do not worry.

A story taken from *None of These Diseases* proves the crippling power of worry.

In the crash of 1929, J.C. Penney's business was solid but he had made some unwise personal commitments. He became so worried that he couldn't sleep. Then he developed "shingles," a disorder that can cause great annoyance and severe pain. He was hospitalized and given sedatives, but got no relief and tossed all night. A combination of circumstances had broken him so completely, physically and mentally, that he was overwhelmed with a fear of death. He wrote farewell letters to his wife and son, for he did not expect to live until morning.

The next morning the great business tycoon heard singing in the hospital chapel. He pulled himself together and entered as the group was singing "God Will Take Care of You." Then followed a Scripture reading and a prayer. In Mr. Penney's own words, "Suddenly something happened. I can't explain it. I can only call it a miracle. I felt as if I had been instantly lifted out of the darkness of a dungeon into warm, brilliant sunlight. I felt as if I had been transported from hell to paradise. I felt the power of God as I had never felt it before. I realized then that I alone was responsible for all my troubles. I know that God with His love was there to help me. From that day to this, my life has been free from worry. I am seventy-one years old, and the most dramatic and glorious minutes of my life were those I spent in that chapel that morning: 'God Will Take Care of You.'"

It is a proven fact that sickness comes not only from Satan, but also from harmful emotion such as fear, worry, hate, envy, and the way we handle pressure. Dr. McMillen states, "The stresses of living are not nearly as responsible for a host of debilitating diseases as are our faulty reactions to those stresses." Wrong actions can also result in accidents which have ramifications of physical weaknesses such as drunken driving, diving in too shallow of water, or smoking.

If you are sick and you can honestly answer, "I have taken all the right steps, not most of them, but all of them," then relax and leave it in God's hands. He, not man, is the healer of all disease. Doctors only dress the wounds; God heals them.

III John 2 gives God's desire for His children. "Beloved, I wish *above all things* that thou mayest prosper and be in *health,* even as thy soul prospereth." Then you ask, "Why do some die from sickness before they live their allotted 70 years?" My answer is this: God is God, and He is in charge. We are finite creatures trying our best to walk according to the Word, but even at our best we sometimes fall short. Whether we are not doing something right, or whether God had a purpose higher than our thoughts--who is to know? It would be foolish for anyone to judge another and say, "They did not have the faith," for only God sees the heart. If this subject causes friction, judging, and resentment, then we best examine our hearts. It is not a subject of arrogance, but one of humility. If we all got what we deserved, we would all perish because of sin. Surely our salvation, healing, and righteousness all comes from the grace and favor of our Lord Jesus Christ.

He is all-knowing, and does not have to ask us if He can do something. He sees things in the future that we do not see. He holds all of eternity in His hands. Paul speaks about death as a gain. "For me to live is Christ, and to die is gain" (Philippians 1:21), but most of us do not want to gain in that way. Psalm 116:15 says, "Precious in the sight of the Lord is the death of his saints," but we hope that preciousness will be reserved for our later years. We all want to live, and that is good. Something would be wrong with us if we desired death.

We will never understand some things. Why does a baby die? Why does a precious saint die early, while a crusty, old, hardened sinner lives until he is almost petrified? We just have to leave it in God's hands, do the best we can, and humbly try to build a good relationship with God and others, for the whole law rests on these two commandments: love God first, and your neighbor second. It does not matter where sickness originates from; we must try to keep our minds focused on God and not on the disease, for God is all-powerful and mighty in battle. He can heal, no matter what! Remember the Word when you are sick. "According to your faith be it unto thee" (Matthew 9:29). Have faith in God!

My hope is that this book will generate new faith to believe in God to do greater things among us. We do not need anymore condemnation. God forbid! We all need to be encouraged and to encourage one another in the Lord and with His precious Word. Let us do everything we can do and leave the miracle with the Lord. Remember what the angel told Mary: "For with God nothing shall be impossible" (Luke 1:37).

One last word on this subject. According to the scripture, the prayer of faith shall save the sick, and by His stripes we were healed. This is an absolute! The same promise that promises healing for sickness and disease cannot always be applied to circumstances or fiery trials. Two examples of this are the three Hebrew children and John the Baptist.

When the three Hebrew children were promised death, notice their faith. The king asked them if their God would deliver them out of his hands. They answered,

> If it be so, our God whom we serve is able to deliver us from the burning fiery furnace, and he will deliver us out of thine hand, O King. But if not, be it known unto thee, O King, that we will not serve thy gods, nor worship the golden image which thou hast set up (Daniel 3:17-18).

God did deliver them with a great miracle. No fire was smelled on their clothes, their hair was not singed, and He walked in the fire with them.

On the other hand, John the Baptist was in prison and sent word to Jesus and asked, "Art thou the Christ, or do we seek for another?" He was asking in so many words, "Are you going to get me out of this prison?"

> Jesus answered and said unto them, Go and shew John again those things which ye do hear and see: The blind receive their sight, and the lame walk, the lepers are cleansed, and the deaf hear, the dead are

raised up, and the poor have the gospel preached to them. And blessed is he, whosoever shall not be offended in me (Matthew 11:4-6).

Jesus was telling him to believe and keep his faith, even if he was not delivered out of prison. No matter what God does concerning your circumstances, it is better to die with faith in God, as John the Baptist did, than to live in doubt.

Stephen, the first martyr of the church, died so that Saul could see the glory of the Lord and be saved shortly thereafter. Though we would call this Stephen's "non-deliverance," half the known world embraced the gospel of Christ through Paul's ministry as a result of his first glimpse of true Christianity.

Keep your faith in God in all things. God is God and beside Him there is none other. He will do great and mighty things, but His ways are not always our ways. The thing to do is to always stand on His word and trust Him explicitly. He does care about each of His children, and His heart is touched with their feelings, tears, and times of troubles. If you will go to Him, He will never leave you nor forsake you, but He will be with you until the end of the world.

Chapter 17
Instrument of Faith

In the Ocean Grove Auditorium there was advertised a concert by a Master violinist to be played on a five-thousand dollar violin accompanied by the pipe organ, one of the greatest in the land.

At the appointed time a tremendous crowd was present with high anticipations. The mighty organ pealed forth a fitting background for the masterful player.

As he put the instrument to his shoulder and drew the bow across the strings a rich, deep, sweet mellow tone floated out upon the air. His great soul pulsed forth a glorious message of power and inspiration. As he proceeded the music grew in volume and sweetness. So majestic was it that it seemed that the whole auditorium was vibrant with the tide of resonance.

As the Master came to his brilliant and sublime climax, completing his rendition, there was at first a breathless stillness. Then there burst forth a tremendous storm of applause. The people cheered and cheered. They arose to their feet and cheered on and on. Right in the midst of this almost riotous expression of delight the Master stepped to the front of the platform and bringing the violin down upon the table smashed it into a thousand pieces.

The audience amazed and all but dazed sat down aghast. What could it mean? Had the Master had such an inspiration of music that it had dethroned his reason? Had he gone mad under the inspiration? While the crowd was thus sitting in perfect amazement the great violinist walked to the other end of the platform, and opening another violin case, took out another instrument. He walked to the center of the stage and holding up the instrument said, "The instrument upon which I have just been playing, now in splinters, cost $2.69." Then holding up the instrument in his hand said, "This is the $5000 violin." It was not the instrument that caused the beautiful music, it was the Master musician.

God is looking for instruments he can play beautiful music upon or through. "Neither yield ye your members as instruments of unrighteousness unto sin; but yield yourselves unto God, as those that are alive from the dead, and your members as instruments of righteousness unto God" (Romans 6:13).

All He needs is a willing heart. He used a little boy's lunch of five loaves of bread and two fishes and fed over 5,000 people. What a miracle, because of the availability of what the boy had in his hand. He used a man, Moses, who thought he could not talk very well, and therefore was reluctant, but finally was willing. Because of his willingness, he delivered a nation from Pharaoh's harsh rule.

He used a little nameless girl in Naaman's household to be instrumental in causing him to be healed. She let her faith talk even in a heathen land. He can work wonders through a yielded instrument, for it is not the instrument that plays--it is the Master that causes the music to burst forth. When Jesus spoke He said, "...Have faith in God..." (Mark 11:22). Faith in the Master, not the vessel. It is the power of God that does the miracle.

When Elijah was on Mount Carmel and the great manifestation of fire from heaven filled the sky and then consumed the sacrifice, the people recognized the miracle of the Master and cried, "The Lord He is God!"

The instrument does not have to be a $5000 one, it can be a $2.69 one.

Chang was a very humble Christian, but he was an instrument of faith. He was undersized, stoop shouldered, partly deaf, and halting in speech, yet he was a battery of power through prayer.

He wanted to bring the really big men of his village into touch with Christ. He had no money, no influence, so he prayed steadily for nearly a year. He prayed that on a given date a band of Bible women might return to his village, and also for the presence of the foreign pastor and several native evangelists. They all came.

He prayed that a crowd of heathen might leave their spring plowing, dragging and sowing and come to listen to the teaching. They came.

There was no building large enough to hold the crowd he wanted to see gathered, so he prayed for a big revival tent to be sent. It came.

The people of a neighboring village brought all that was needed, and put seats and lamps in position. These meetings resulted in more than 3,000 men hearing the gospel and in the local people paying all expenses.

After the meeting Chang felt the need of a Christian school and teacher. He prayed and got both.

He had long prayed for the conversion of his old mother. She was converted. He had especially prayed for favorable weather during the meeting. He got it.

According to his prevailing prayer and faith it all came to pass, and many souls were brought to the Lord Jesus Christ.

There are different ways to be an instrument the Master can work through, but He desires to work through every Christian. Miracles are waiting to happen, souls are waiting to be saved, songs are waiting to be written and sung, books are waiting to be written and read, messages are waiting to be dug out and delivered, hearts are waiting to be ministered to in faith. So many needs and hungry hearts are waiting to be lifted up from the normal into the realm of the rapturous music of faith in God.

The Master is waiting; where are the instruments? When Jesus was at the wedding in Cana, and they ran out of wine, His mother told Him to perform a miracle. He was not ready, but she just ignored Him and turned to the servants and said to them, "...Whatsoever he saith unto you, do it" (John 2:5). That is how all the miracles started. They simply obeyed the Master, and He performed the miracle. It is Him flowing through the vessel, not the vessel performing the miracle. The vessels are empty of self, but full of Him.

Historians tell us that George Mueller had great faith, and that he had over 25,000 miracles take place in his life. He was a man of much prayer and prayed several times throughout the day. He said, "There was a day when I died, utterly died, to George Mueller, his opinions, preferences, tastes, and will. I died to the world, its approval or censure: died to the approval or blame even of my brethren and friends and since then I have studied only to show myself approved unto God."

This does not mean that he was arrogant or rebellious to those in authority over him. It simply means that he did not want to be in charge any longer, he wanted the Master to be in charge. That is what Jesus meant when He answered the question of what it took to be a disciple of His. "And he said to them all, If any man will come after me, let him deny himself, and take up his cross daily, and follow me. For whosoever will save his life, shall love it; but whosoever will lose his life for my sake, the same shall save it" (Luke 9:23-24).

It is a releasing of ourselves to the higher purpose of Christ, and allowing His thoughts to become our thoughts. Wrapped up in a nutshell, it is falling in love with Him.

When a group of young people were going to go into the Lord's service, the leader asked them, "And why do you wish to go as a foreign missionary?"

"I want to reach others across the sea because Christ has commanded us to go into all the world and preach the Gospel to every creature," one replied.

Another said, "I want to go because millions are dying without ever having heard of Jesus, the only One who can save them." Others had similar answers.

The leader looked at them thoughtfully for a moment and then said, "All of your motives are good, but I fear they will fail you in times of severe testing and tribulation--especially if you are confronted with the possibility of having to face death for your testimony. The only motive that will enable you to remain true is stated in II Corinthians 5:14. Christ's love constraining you will keep you faithful in every situation."

This is what it is all about. The vessels must be so in love that they want to help other people find this love. The secrets and answers they have found sings in their soul until it bursts forth into a melody of song. They have light, and they want others to light their candles at their flame. Jesus said, "Neither do men light a candle, and put it under a bushel, but on a candlestick; and it giveth light unto all that are in the house. Let your light so shine before men, that they may see your good works, and glorify your Father which is in heaven" (Matthew 5:15-16).

WHAT'S IT TO BE?
by Joy Haney

What's it to be?
Will you glorify or grumble?
Will you save or make others stumble?
Will you love or hate?
Will you lift up or berate?

GREAT FAITH

What's it to be?
The choice is your own.
You can groan and moan.
Say it is too much work.
Walk by opportunity and shirk.

What's it to be?
Will your life sing and shine?
Will you be caring and kind?
You have the power to place yourself in His hands,
Heaven is watching and waiting in the grandstands.

What's it to be?
Will you say yes and give the Saviour your best,
So others can have life and find sweet rest?
Will you be that instrument and willingly give,
So the world can hear beautiful music and live?

BIBLIOGRAPHY

Collins, Gary R. *Your Magnificent Mind.* Grand Rapids, Michigan: Baker Book House, 1988.

Gibbon, Edward. *The Decline and Fall of the Roman Empire.* New York: Washington Square Press, 1962.

God Answers Prayer. Compiled by Mary Wallace. Hazelwood, Missouri: Word Aflame Press, 1986.

Lake, Alexander. *Your Prayers Are Always Answered.* New York: Simon and Schuster, 1956.

Tan, Paul Lee. *Encyclopedia of 7,700 Illustrations: Signs of the Times.* Rockville, Maryland: Assurance Publishers, 1979.

Wigglesworth, Smith. *Ever Increasing Faith.* Springfield, Missouri: Gospel Publishing House, 1924, revised 1971.